W9-AZF-671

Contents

Name _____

Trace over the numbers.

Color the correct number of objects in each row.

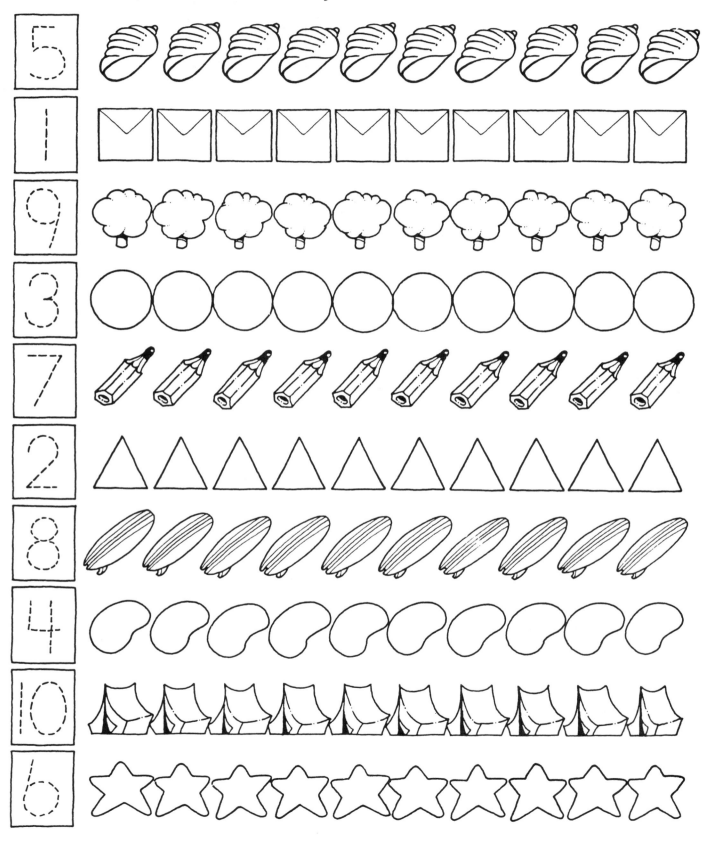

Topic 1: Investigating Numbers

Write the missing numbers.

Draw cherries on the empty plates.

Trace over the numbers.

1

3 4 6

2 9

Name _____

Here are some numbers to copy.

Fill in the empty cards.

Draw the missing eggs.

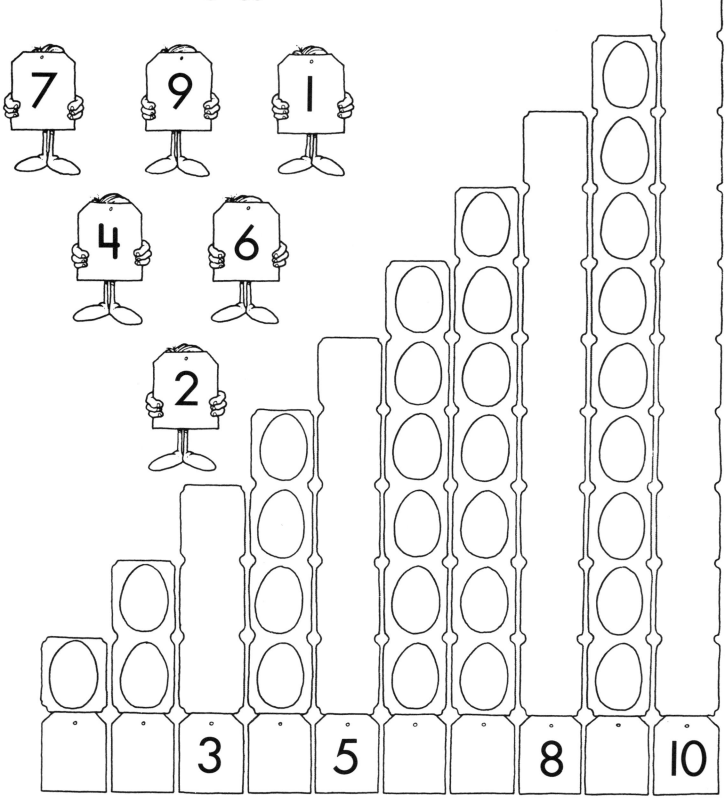

Topic 1: Investigating Numbers

Name _____

Write the number on each card.

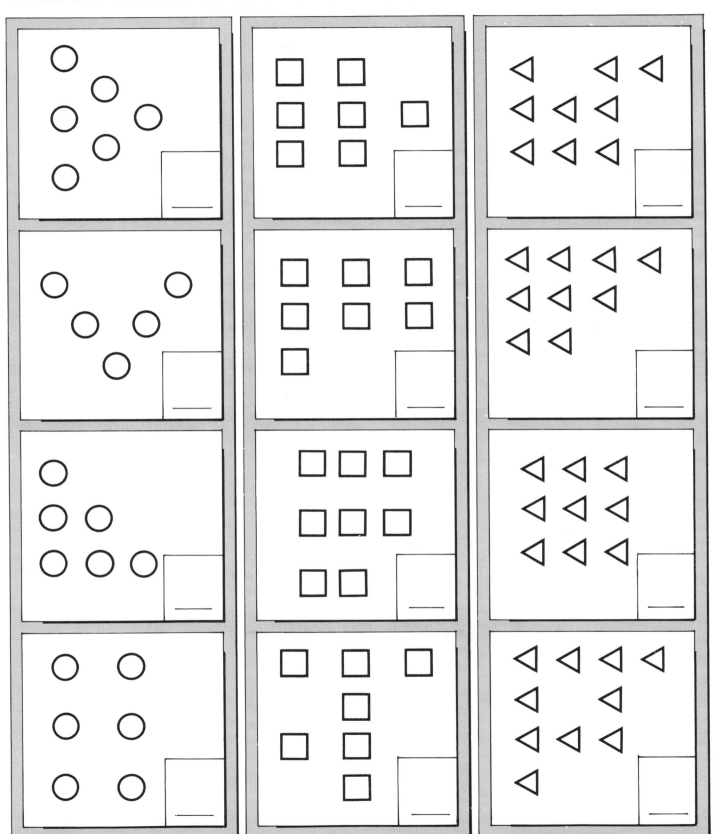

On each strip, put a check on the card that does not belong.

Name _____

Use an orange rod to find the pictures that are the same length.
Color them orange.

Name _____

Estimate which containers in your collection
might hold the same amount as the mug.
Measure each.
Draw the containers which hold about the
same amount as the mug.

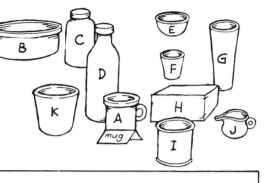

These hold about the same amount
as the mug.

Name _____

Count the toys.   Color one group of toys in each picture.
Write the numbers.

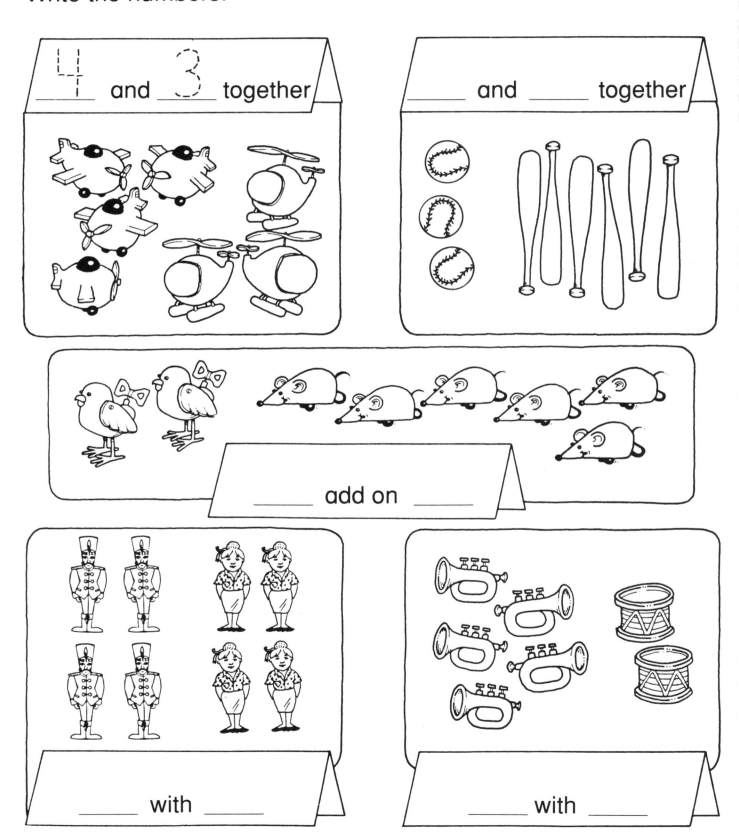

4 and 3 together

_____ and _____ together

_____ add on _____

_____ with _____

_____ with _____

Name _____

Count and add more drawings.

Write the numbers.

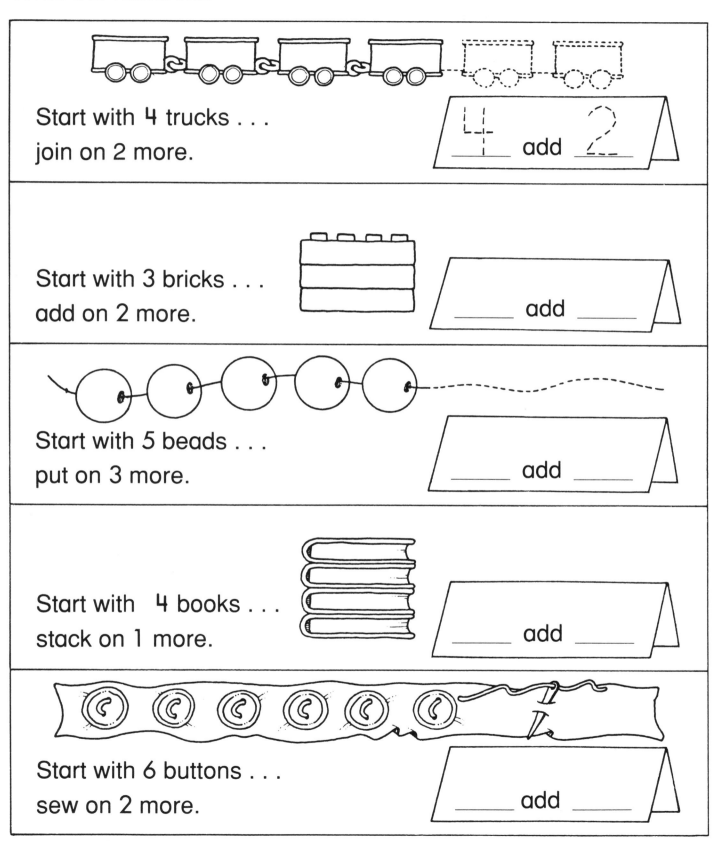

Start with 4 trucks . . .
join on 2 more.

4 add 2

Start with 3 bricks . . .
add on 2 more.

_____ add _____

Start with 5 beads . . .
put on 3 more.

_____ add _____

Start with 4 books . . .
stack on 1 more.

_____ add _____

Start with 6 buttons . . .
sew on 2 more.

_____ add _____

Name _____

Read, count, and add more drawings.
Write the numbers.

Count the cats. Add 1 more.

 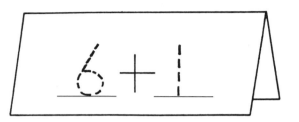

$6 + 1$

Count the flowers. Add 4 more.

 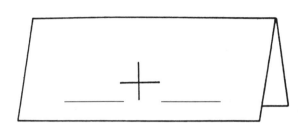

___ + ___

Count the marbles. Add 4 more.

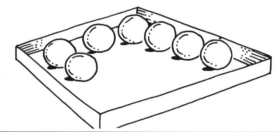 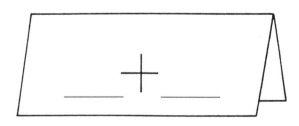

___ + ___

Count the apples. Add 4 more.

 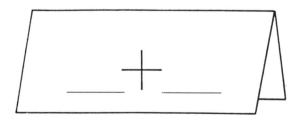

___ + ___

Count the leaves. Add 3 more.

 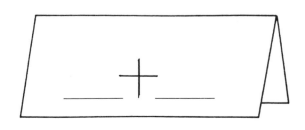

___ + ___

12

Name _____

Count. Write the numbers.
Color in each part of the puzzles.

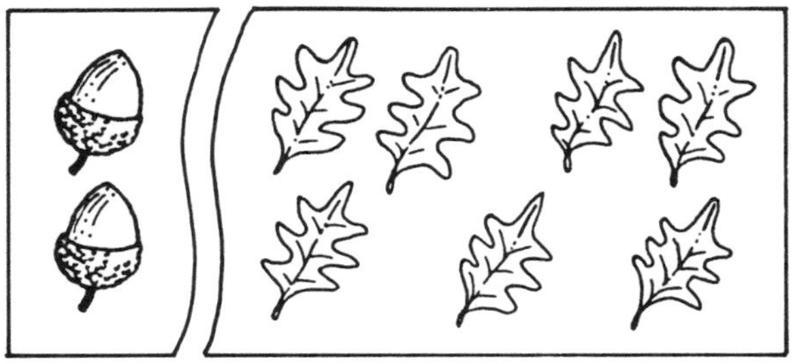

$2 + 7$

___ + ___

___ + ___

___ + ___

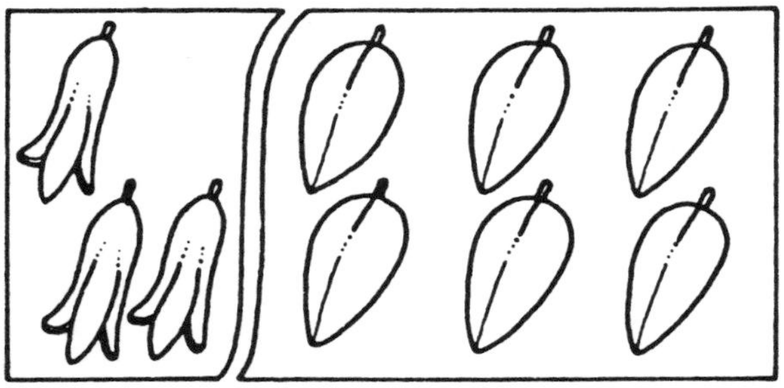

___ + ___

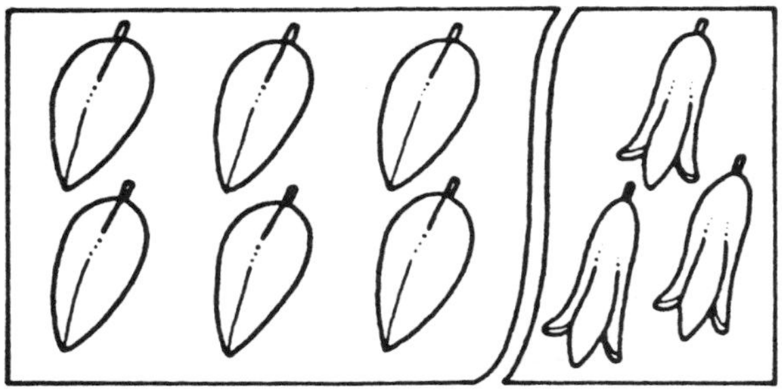

___ + ___

Name _____

Use 2 colors to show the different things in each balloon.
Write the numbers.

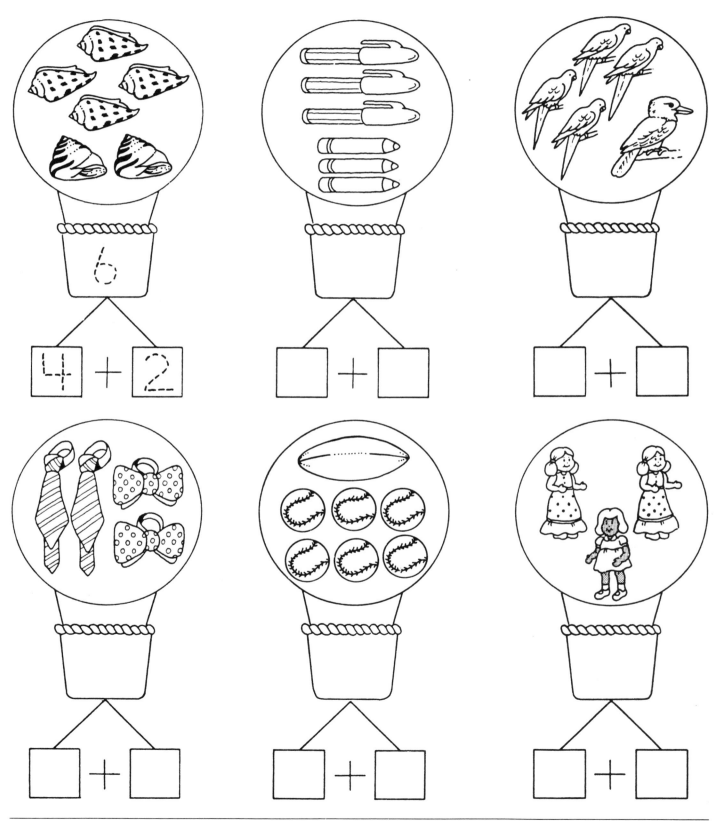

Name _____

Count the clothespins
on this side.
    Write the numbers.

On this side, draw a check
for each pin.
    Write the number.

3 + 4 〈 is equal to 〉 ✓ ✓ ✓ ✓ ✓ ✓ ✓ 7

___ + ___ 〈 is equal to 〉 ___

___ + ___ 〈 is equal to 〉 ___

___ + ___ 〈 = 〉 ___

___ + ___ 〈 = 〉 ___

___ + ___ 〈 = 〉 ___

Topic 4: Addition Sentences

15

Name _____

Add to find the answer.		Three balls add one ball. ◎◎◎ ◎	$\begin{array}{r} 3 \\ +1 \\ \hline 4 \end{array}$
	Draw a picture.		Write an addition fact.
Three balls add five balls.			$\begin{array}{r} 3 \\ +5 \\ \hline 8 \end{array}$
Four pens add two pens.			
Six dolls add two dolls.			
Three bats add four bats.			
Eight flags add one flag.			

How many shells will be in each pail?

Count on 1, 2, or 3 to find the answer. Write each addition fact.

Count on 1, 2, or 3 to find the answers.

8
+ 3
11

6
+ 2
8

7
+ 1
8

9
+ 2
11

1
+ 8
9

2
+ 7
9

6
+ 1
7

1
+ 9
10

Topic 5: Addition Fact Strategies - counting on

17

Measure the fish picture. Then write the numbers.

The fish is about as long as _____ clothespins.

The fish is about as long as _____ paper clips.

The fish is about as long as _____ connecting cubes.

The fish is about as long as _____ washers.

The fish is about as long as _____ cubes.

The children will need the items listed for measuring.

Topic 6: Measurement - using non-standard units

Name _____

Measure each picture with cubes.
Then write the numbers.

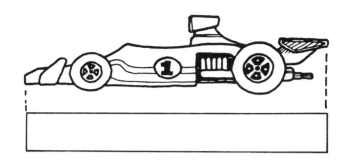

The car is _____ cubes long.

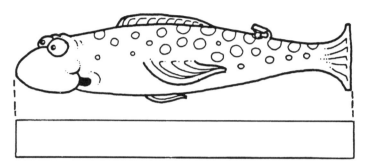

The fish is _____ cubes long.

The bear is _____ cubes tall.

The dog is _____ cubes long.

The soldier is _____ cubes tall.

The children will need white Cuisenaire rods for measuring.

Topic 6: Measurement - using non-standard units

19

Name _____

The jar holds as much as . . .

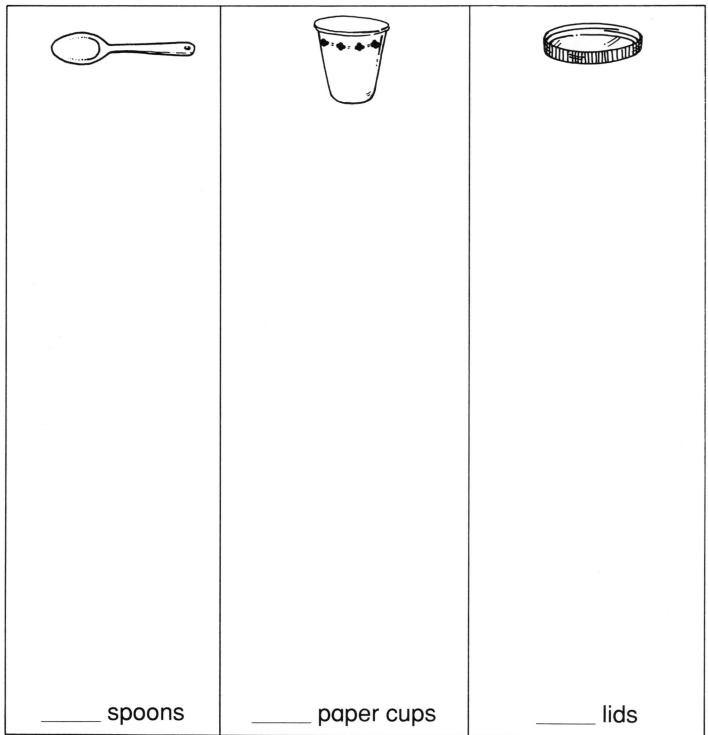

_____ spoons	_____ paper cups	_____ lids

The children will need a jar, a spoon, a paper cup and a lid for this measuring activity.

Topic 6: Measurement - using non-standard units

Name _____

Use the number strip to help find the answers.

| 1 | 2 | 3 | 4 | 5 | 6 | 7 | 8 | 9 | 10 | 11 |

Start at 5
Count on 1

$$\begin{array}{r} 5 \\ +\,1 \\ \hline \end{array}$$

Start at 5
Count on 2

$$\begin{array}{r} 5 \\ +\,2 \\ \hline \end{array}$$

Start at 5
Count on 3

$$\begin{array}{r} 5 \\ +\,3 \\ \hline \end{array}$$

Start at 6
Count on 1

$$\begin{array}{r} 6 \\ +\,1 \\ \hline \end{array}$$

Start at 6
Count on 2

$$\begin{array}{r} 6 \\ +\,2 \\ \hline \end{array}$$

Start at 6
Count on 3

$$\begin{array}{r} 6 \\ +\,3 \\ \hline \end{array}$$

Start at 7
Count on 1

$$\begin{array}{r} 7 \\ +\,1 \\ \hline \end{array}$$

Start at 7
Count on 2

$$\begin{array}{r} 7 \\ +\,2 \\ \hline \end{array}$$

Start at 7
Count on 3

$$\begin{array}{r} 7 \\ +\,3 \\ \hline \end{array}$$

Start at 8
Count on 1

$$\begin{array}{r} 8 \\ +\,1 \\ \hline \end{array}$$

Start at 8
Count on 2

$$\begin{array}{r} 8 \\ +\,2 \\ \hline \end{array}$$

Start at 8
Count on 3

$$\begin{array}{r} 8 \\ +\,3 \\ \hline \end{array}$$

Add one more shape to the patterns which have only 10 pieces.
Write the numbers.

Topic 7: Patterning, Grouping, Partitioning - 11 to 15

Name _____

In each picture, color 10 flowers blue and any others red.

Match the numbers to the groups of 12.

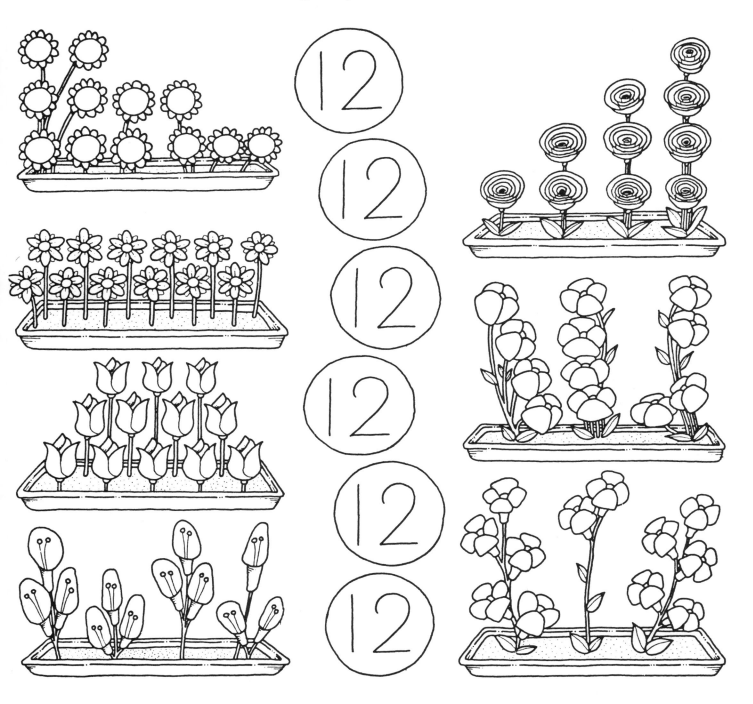

Draw or paste 12 flowers here.

Write the missing numbers.

| 1 | | 3 | | 5 | | 7 | | 9 | | 11 | 12 |

| 1 | 2 | | 4 | 5 | | 7 | 8 | | 10 | 11 | 12 |

| 1 | 2 | 3 | | 5 | 6 | 7 | | 9 | 10 | 11 | 12 |

Write the number altogether. Color groups of two.

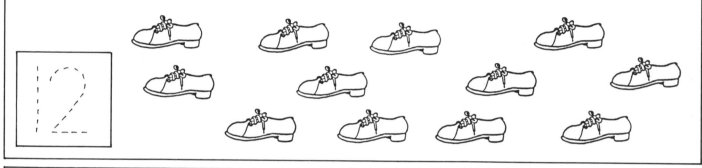

Write the number altogether. Color groups of three.

Write the number altogether. Color groups of four.

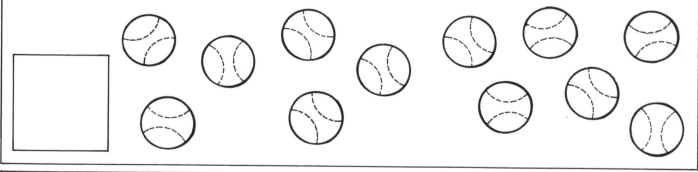

Topic 7: Patterning, Grouping, Partitioning - 11 to 15

Name _____

Use an egg carton and beads to help with the number stories
on this page.

Start with beads that are all the same color.

Add more in a different color to make 12.

Add more beads to make 12. Write the missing number.	Turn the carton around. Write a new story using +.
Start with 11. $11 + \underline{} = 12$	$1 + \underline{11} = 12$
Start with 10. $10 + \underline{} = 12$	
Start with 9. $9 + \underline{} = 12$	
Start with 8. $8 + \underline{} = 12$	
Start with 7. $7 + \underline{} = 12$	

Start with 6. How many more to make 12? _____

Name _____

Draw the hand on each clock face.

Draw a picture to match each story.

At 7 o'clock I get up.		
At 8 o'clock I eat breakfast.		
At 9 o'clock I start school.		
At 12 o'clock I eat lunch.		
At 4 o'clock I get home from school.		
At 6 o'clock I eat dinner.		

Topic 7: Patterning, Grouping, Partitioning - 11 to 15

Name _____

Color 10 things in each picture.
Write the number in all.

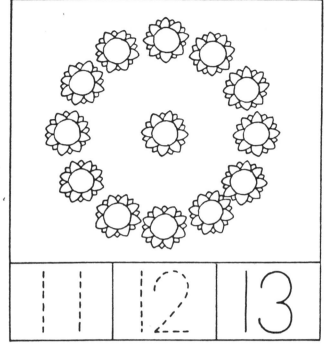

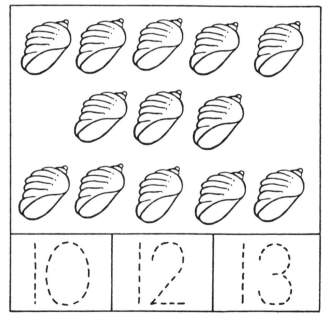

Draw 13 beads on the string. Color 10.

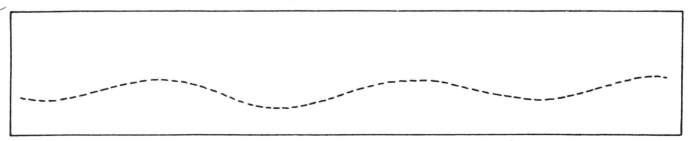

Write all the missing numbers.

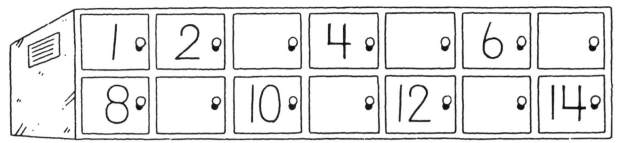

There are _____ doors in all.

Color 10 glasses orange.

Draw one straw
for each glass.

Color 10 pieces of fruit on each tray.

There are _____
pieces of fruit
on this tray.

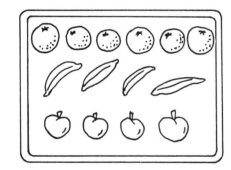

There are _____ pieces of fruit
on this tray.

Draw 14 balloons. Color 10 of them.

Topic 7: Patterning, Grouping, Partitioning - 11 to 15

Name _____

Draw 2 legs on each bird.

Write the number of legs.

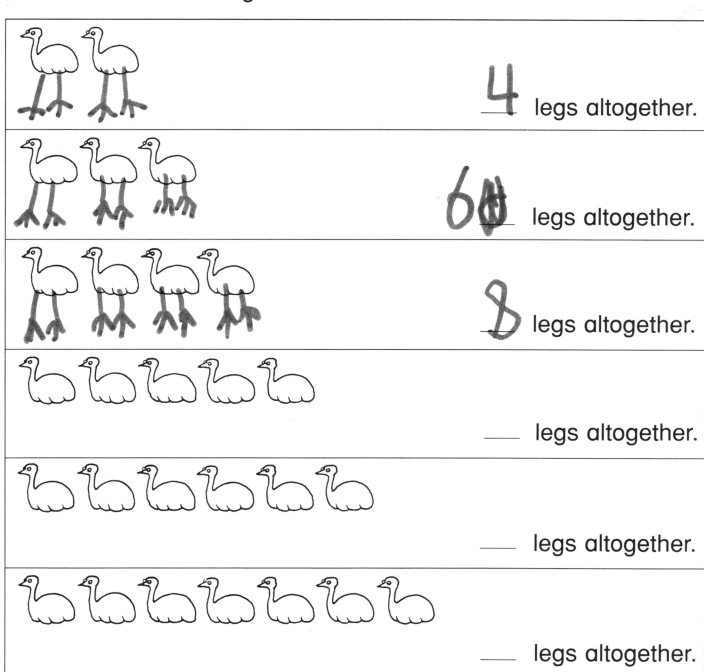

4 legs altogether.

6 legs altogether.

8 legs altogether.

____ legs altogether.

____ legs altogether.

____ legs altogether.

Write the missing numbers.

Color the first 10 squares.

| 1 | 2 | 3 | 4 | 5 | 6 | 7 | 8 | 9 | 10 | 11 | 12 | 13 | 14 |

Ring twos.
Count by twos.
Write the numbers.

Ring twos.   Write the numbers.

Write the numbers.   Join the boxes in the correct order.

Topic 7: Patterning, Grouping, Partitioning - 11 to 15

Name _____

Color in the patterns.

In each row, write the number in all.

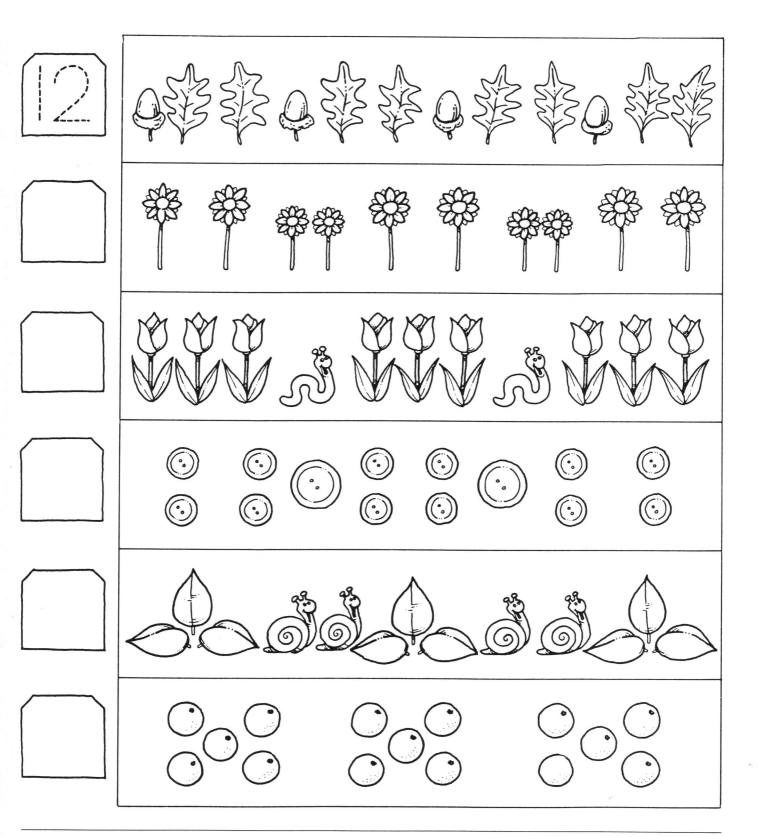

Name _____

Write the missing numbers.

| 1 | | 3 | | 5 | | 7 | | 9 | | 11 | | | 13 | | 15 |

| 1 | 2 | | 4 | 5 | | 7 | 8 | | 10 | 11 | | | 13 | 14 | |

| 1 | 2 | 3 | 4 | | 6 | 7 | 8 | 9 | | 11 | 12 | 13 | 14 |

Ring groups of 3.

Write what happened. _____

_____

Ring groups of 5.

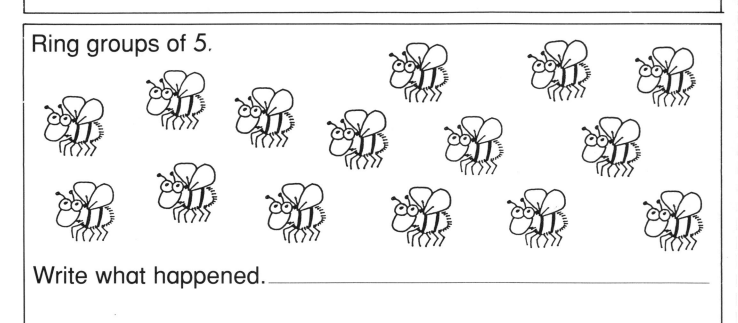

Write what happened. _____

_____

Topic 7: Patterning, Grouping, Partitioning - 11 to 15

Name _____

Color the first 10 beads green.
Color the last 5 beads yellow.

Write the answers.

4 + 1 = ____   3 + 2 = ____   2 + 3 = ____   1 + 4 = ____

14 + 1 = ____   13 + 2 = ____   12 + 3 = ____   11 + 4 = ____

Color each picture to match the facts.

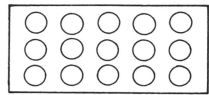

9 + 6 = ____   6 + 9 = ____

8 + 7 = ____   7 + 8 = ____

Write the missing numbers.

| 2 | 4 | 6 | 8 | 10 | 12 | 14 | |

4 +1	14 +1	2 +3	12 +3	3 +2	13 +2	1 +4	11 +4
10 +5	5 +10	9 +6	6 +9	7 +8	8 +7	15 +0	0 +15

Color the squares blue.

Color the rectangles red.

Color the triangles green.

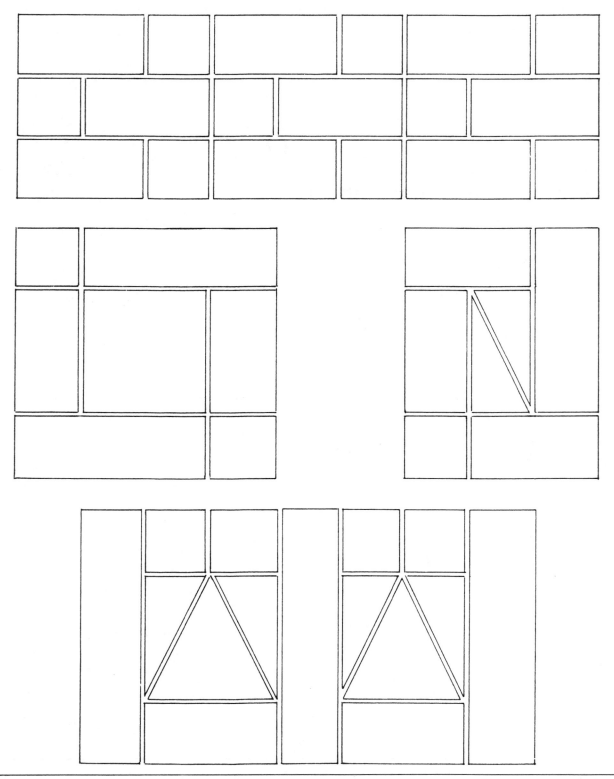

Draw a line to join the ovals that have the same pattern.

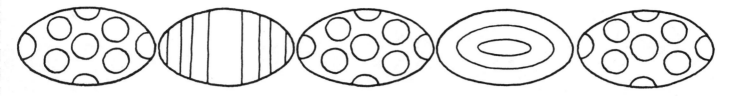

Draw a different pattern inside each empty oval.

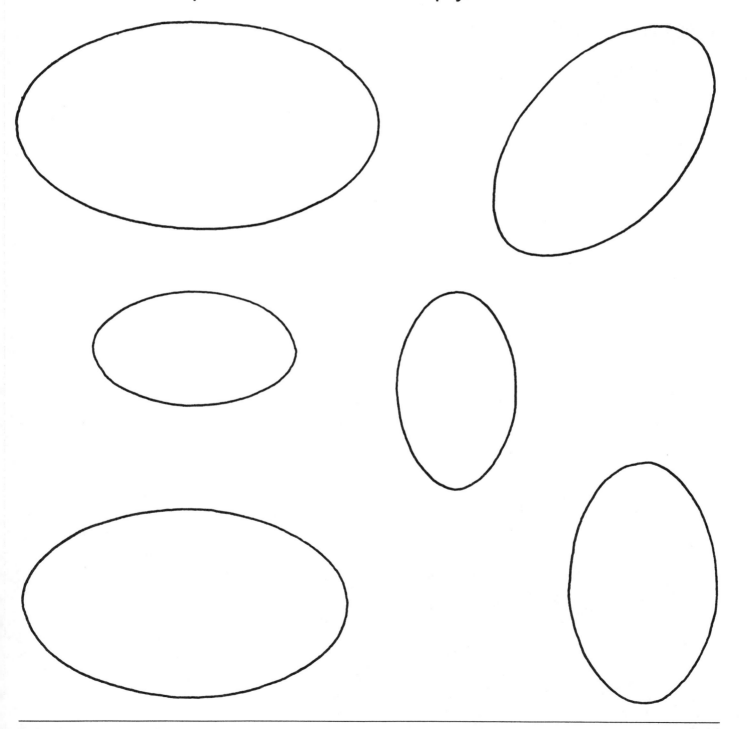

Name _____

Draw a line to join the diamonds that have the same pattern.

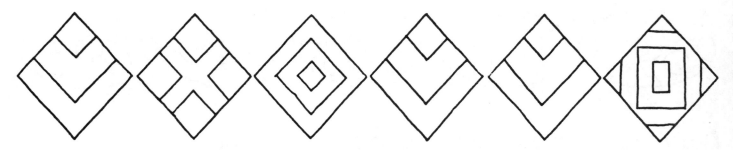

Make a different pattern inside each empty diamond.

Topic 8: Investigating Shapes

Name _____

Write the numbers.

Here are _____ shapes.   Here are _____ shapes.

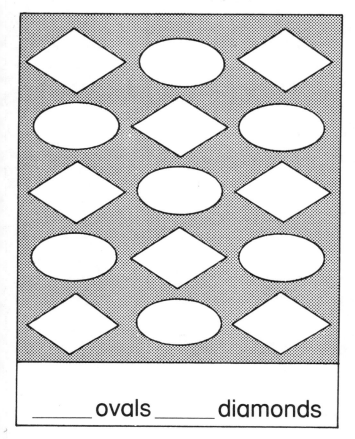

_____ ovals _____ diamonds

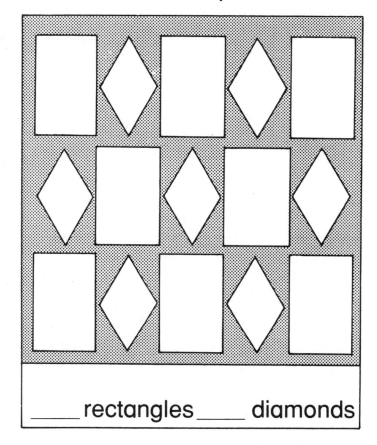

_____ rectangles _____ diamonds

I counted _____ diamonds altogether.

Draw a pattern with 15 shapes.

Draw a line from each X to the shape that belongs in that place.
Color the 4-sided shapes red.

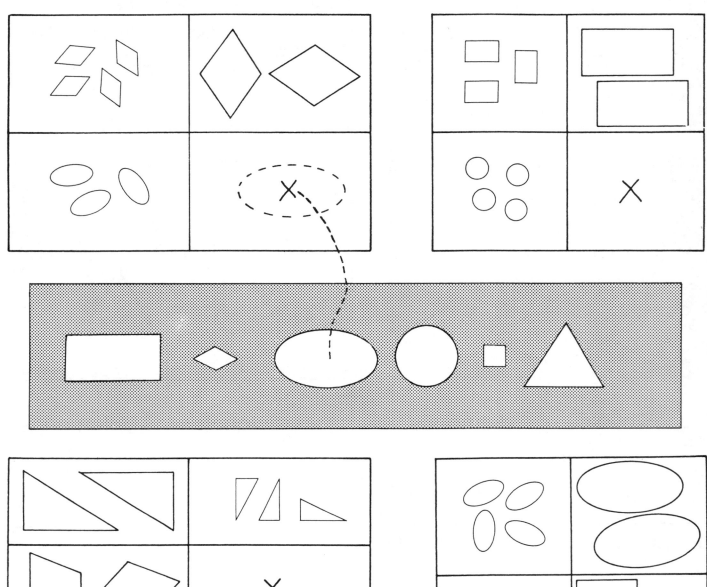

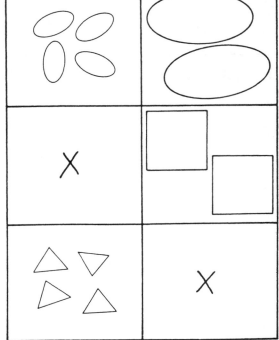

Topic 8: Investigating Shapes

Name _____

Write the numbers. Color the things that are left.

Start with 6.
2 hop away.

_____ take away _____

 Start with 5.
3 fall down.

_____ take away _____

Start with 6.
I jumps off.

_____ take away _____

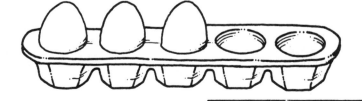

Start with 5.
Cook 2.

_____ take away _____

Name _____

Use different colors for each set.

Ring sets of 2.

How many trucks? _____

Ring sets of 4.

How many boats? _____

Ring sets of 8.

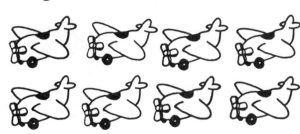 

How many planes? _____

Draw 16 tents.

Ring 10 tents.

Topic 10: Patterning, Grouping, Partitioning - 16 to 19

Name _____

Draw dots to double the number.   Write the double.

Double 2 is _____   Double 4 is _____   Double 8 is _____

Draw 4 sticks.
Ring 2 equal groups.

Draw 8 sticks.
Ring 2 equal groups.

Draw 16 sticks.
Ring 2 equal groups.

Write the missing numbers.

| 1 | 2 | | 4 | 5 | | 7 | 8 | | 10 | 11 | | | 13 | 14 | | | 16 |

Name _____

Color the first 10 dots green.
Color the other dots yellow.

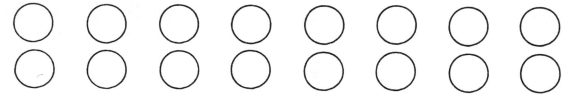

Write 4 number sentences about the dots. Use "add" or "take."

_____   _____

_____   _____

Write the answers. Use the dots to help.

$9 + 1 + 6 =$ _____   16 take 6 = _____

$9 +$ _____ $= 16$ 16 take 7 = _____

$7 + 3 + 6 =$ _____   16 take 10 = _____

$7 +$ _____ $= 16$ 16 take 9 = _____

Write the answers.

5 +1	15 +1	4 +2	14 +2	3 +3	13 +3
2 +4	12 +4	1 +5	11 +5	6 +0	16 +0

Name _____

Write the correct number. Color 10 blocks in each row.

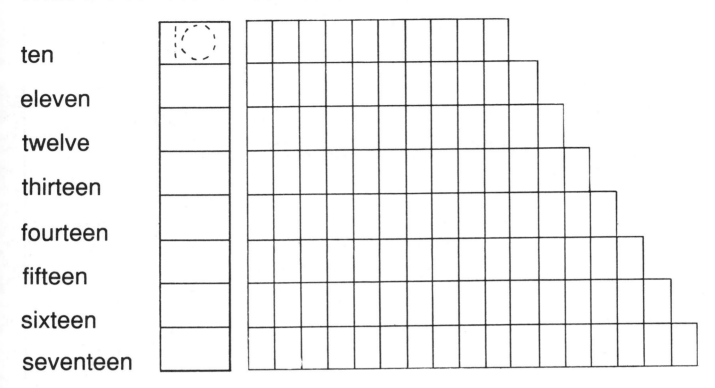

ten
eleven
twelve
thirteen
fourteen
fifteen
sixteen
seventeen

Draw more things to make 17. Trace over the number.

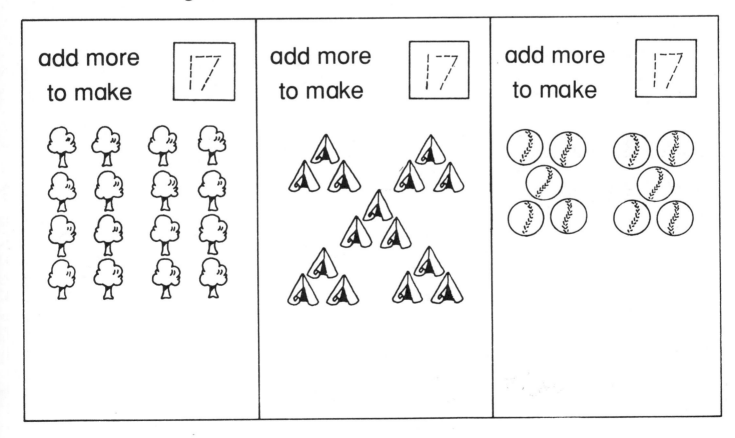

add more to make [17]

add more to make [17]

add more to make [17]

Name _____

Color 10 circles.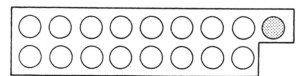

Double 8 is _____

8 + 9 = _____   9 + 8 = _____   Double 8 and 1 more is _____

Make up 4 more addition stories about 17.

_____ _____ _____ _____

Write the answers. Use the circles to check.

10 + 7 = _____   11 + 6 = _____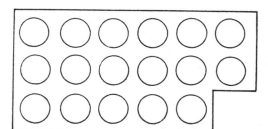

12 + 5 = _____   13 + 4 = _____

14 + 3 = _____   15 + 2 = _____

Write the missing numbers.

| 1 | 2 | | 4 | 5 | | 7 | 8 | | 10 | 11 | |

| 13 | 14 | | 16 | 17 |

Write the answers for these.

2 12	2 12	5 15	5 15
+1 +1	+2 +2	+1 +1	+2 +2
4 14	4 14	3 13	3 13
+1 +1	+2 +2	+1 +1	+2 +2

44

Name _____

Draw 18 balls on each tray. Write the numbers.

Ring groups of 2. There are _____ groups of 2.

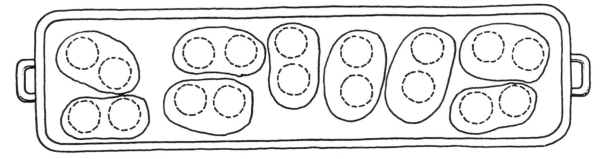

Ring groups of 3. There are _____ groups of 3.

Ring groups of 6. There are _____ groups of 6.

Ring groups of 9. There are _____ groups of 9.

Color 10 △ green.

There are _____ △ altogether.

Color 10 ⬡ red.

There are _____ ⬠ altogether.

Color 10 ▱ blue.

There are _____ ▱ altogether.

Topic 10: Patterning, Grouping, Partitioning - 16 to 19

Name _____

Color 10 circles.

| 1 | 2 | 3 | 4 | 5 | 6 | 7 | 8 | 9 | 10 | 11 | 12 | 13 | 14 | 15 | 16 | 17 | 18 | 19 |

One more than 18 is _____   One less than 18 is _____

The number between 16 and 18 is _____

10 + _____ is 18   8 + _____ is 18   9 + _____ is 18

Use the number strip to help with these.

7 + 1 = _____   6 + 2 = _____   5 + 3 = _____

17 + 1 = _____   16 + 2 = _____   15 + 3 = _____

4 + 4 = _____   3 + 5 = _____   2 + 6 = _____

14 + 4 = _____   13 + 5 = _____   2 + 16 = _____

Write the answers.

| 4 | 5 | 8 | 7 | 3 | 6 | 4 | 6 |
| +1 | +2 | +1 | +1 | +5 | +2 | +2 | +1 |

| 2 | 1 | 8 | 6 | 1 | 2 | 4 | 2 |
| +6 | +7 | +2 | +3 | +9 | +8 | +3 | +5 |

Topic 10: Patterning, Grouping, Partitioning - 16 to 19

47

Ring sets of 2. Write the numbers.

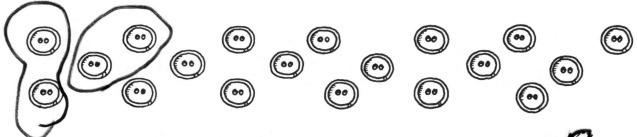

_____ sets of 2 and _____ left over. _____

Ring sets of 3. Write the numbers.

_____ sets of 3 and _____ left over. _____

Ring sets of 4. Write the numbers.

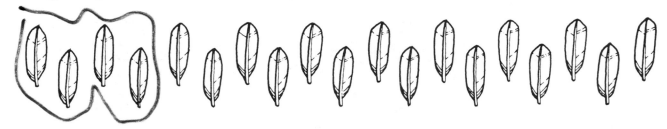

_____ sets of 4 and _____ left over. _____

Ring sets of 5. Write the numbers.

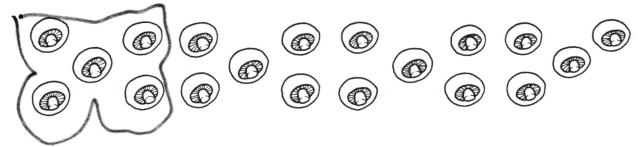

_____ sets of 5 and _____ left over. _____

Topic 10: Patterning, Grouping, Partitioning - 16 to 19

Name _____

Color ten squares.

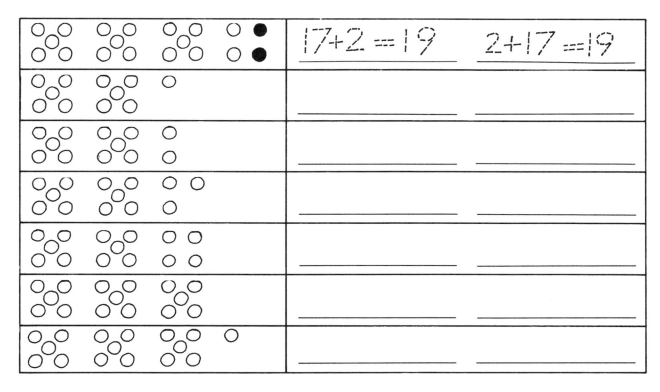

Double 9 is _____

Double 9 add 1 is _____

$10 + 9 =$ _____ $9 +$ _____ $= 19$ $9 + 9 + 1 =$ _____

Add more circles to make 19 in each picture.

Write two addition facts for each picture.

○○○ ○○○ ○○○ ○ ● / ○○○ ○○○ ○○○ ○ ●	$17 + 2 = 19$ $2 + 17 = 19$
○○○ ○○○ ○ / ○○○ ○○○	_____ _____
○○○ ○○○ ○ / ○○○ ○○○ ○	_____ _____
○○○ ○○○ ○ ○ / ○○○ ○○○ ○	_____ _____
○○○ ○○○ ○ ○ / ○○○ ○○○ ○ ○	_____ _____
○○○ ○○○ ○○○ / ○○○ ○○○ ○○○	_____ _____
○○○ ○○○ ○○○ ○ / ○○○ ○○○ ○○○	_____ _____

Color the odd numbers.

1	2	3	4	5	6	7	8	9	10	11	12	13	14	15	16	17	18	19

Write the answers.

8	18	7	17	6	16	5	15
+1	+1	+2	+2	+3	+3	+4	+4

Name _____

Estimate which things weigh about the
same as your math core book.

Check on the balance.

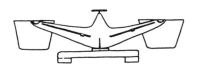

Draw the things that balance the book.

These weigh about the same as the book.

The children will need to use balance scales and a variety of objects, some of which weigh about the same as the Moving Into Math Core Book.

Topic 11: Measurement - using non-standard weights

Name _____

Color all the squares red.

Color all the circles blue.

Color all the triangles green.

Draw the correct number of shapes on the chart.

51

How many shapes in the picture?

squares □									
circles ○									
triangles △									
	1	2	3	4	5	6	7	8	9

Name _____

For each strip, circle enough pennies to exchange with the coins in the purse.

Write the amount.

Put an X on the purse that is worth the most.

_____ ¢   _____ ¢   _____ ¢   _____ ¢

If possible, have the children match the coins in each purse with real or plastic pennies.

Topic 13: Using Money

Name _____

Write the numbers.		Total
I buy	Put coins here.	price

📖 5¢ plus ✏️ 3¢	(8 coins)	8¢
🕊 stamp 4¢ plus ⛵ stamp 1¢		¢
🍎 6¢ plus 🍌 4¢		¢
⭕ 4¢ plus 🎉 4¢		¢

Name _____

Count out pennies. Write the total.

Cost
2¢ each

Total
cost _____¢

Cost
1¢ each

Total
cost _____¢

Cost
3¢ each

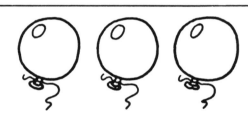

Total
cost _____¢

Cost
5¢ each

Total
cost _____¢

Cost
4¢ each

Total
cost _____¢

54

Name _____

Draw the correct number of beans.

Write the numbers.

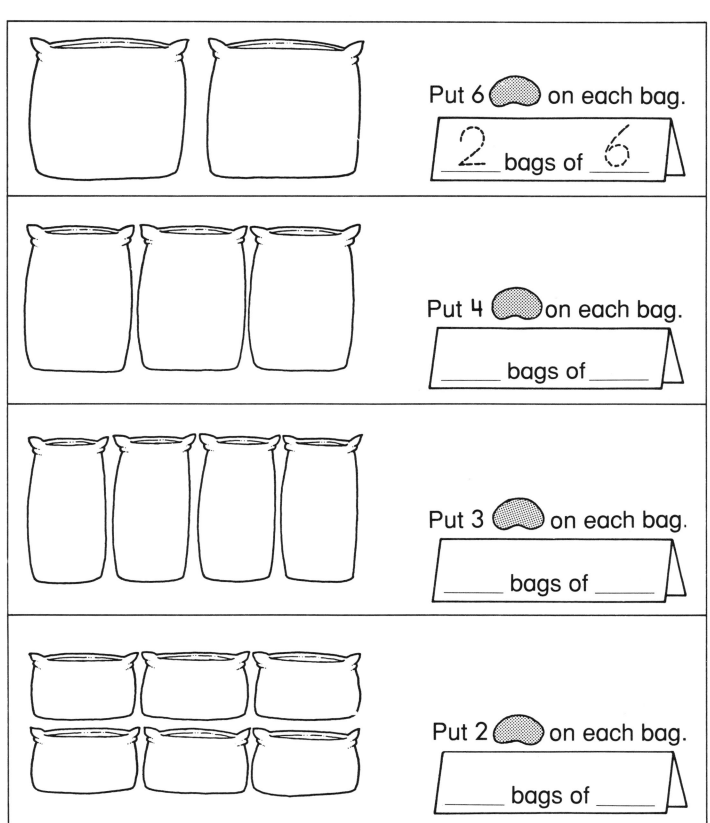

Put 6 🫘 on each bag.

___2___ bags of ___6___

Put 4 🫘 on each bag.

_____ bags of _____

Put 3 🫘 on each bag.

_____ bags of _____

Put 2 🫘 on each bag.

_____ bags of _____

Color each strip with 2 colors.

Then write 2 addition facts for each colored strip.

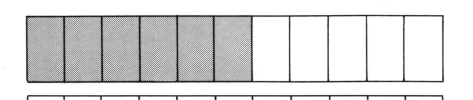

$$\begin{array}{r} 6 \\ + 5 \\ \hline 11 \end{array} \qquad \begin{array}{r} 5 \\ + 6 \\ \hline 11 \end{array}$$

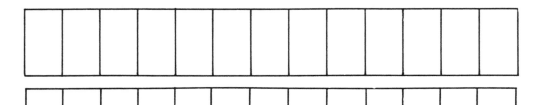

Write the answers for these.

$$\begin{array}{r} 5 \\ + 5 \\ \hline \end{array} \qquad \begin{array}{r} 6 \\ + 6 \\ \hline \end{array} \qquad \begin{array}{r} 7 \\ + 7 \\ \hline \end{array} \qquad \begin{array}{r} 8 \\ + 8 \\ \hline \end{array} \qquad \begin{array}{r} 9 \\ + 9 \\ \hline \end{array} \qquad \begin{array}{r} 10 \\ + 10 \\ \hline \end{array} \qquad \begin{array}{r} 11 \\ + 11 \\ \hline \end{array}$$

Name _____

Draw different pictures of 13 clothespins.
Write 2 addition facts for each picture.

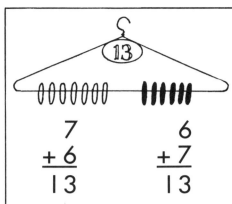

$$\begin{array}{r} 7 \\ +6 \\ \hline 13 \end{array} \qquad \begin{array}{r} 6 \\ +7 \\ \hline 13 \end{array}$$

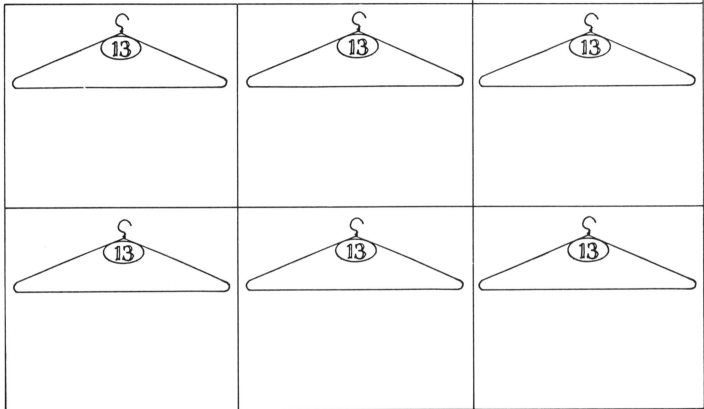

Write the "turnaround fact" for each of these.

Then write the answer for both facts.

$\begin{array}{r} 8 \\ +7 \\ \hline \end{array}$	$\begin{array}{r} 6 \\ +9 \\ \hline \end{array}$	$\begin{array}{r} 7 \\ +5 \\ \hline \end{array}$	$\begin{array}{r} 4 \\ +9 \\ \hline \end{array}$
$\begin{array}{r} 9 \\ +3 \\ \hline \end{array}$	$\begin{array}{r} 8 \\ +2 \\ \hline \end{array}$	$\begin{array}{r} 9 \\ +8 \\ \hline \end{array}$	$\begin{array}{r} 7 \\ +4 \\ \hline \end{array}$

Name _____

Draw different pictures of 17 dots.
Write 2 addition facts for each picture.

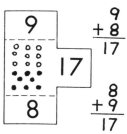

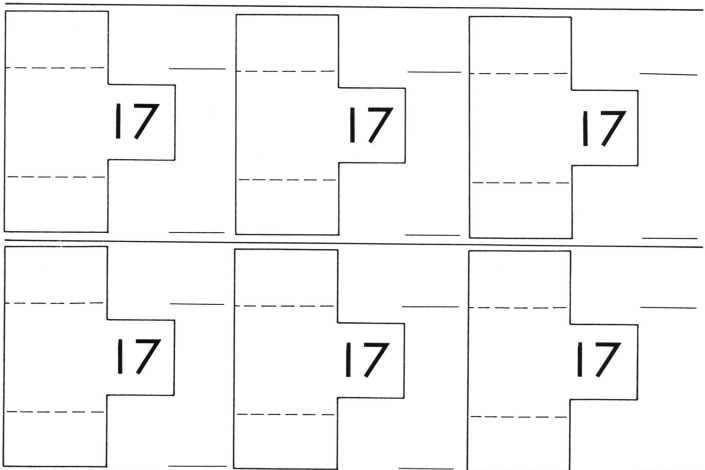

Write addition facts that have 14 as the answer.

+	+	+	+	+	+	+
14	14	14	14	14	14	14

+	+	+	+	+	+	+
14	14	14	14	14	14	14

Topic 15: Problem Solving with Addition - finding combinations

Name _____

Draw dots to double the number.

Write the answers.

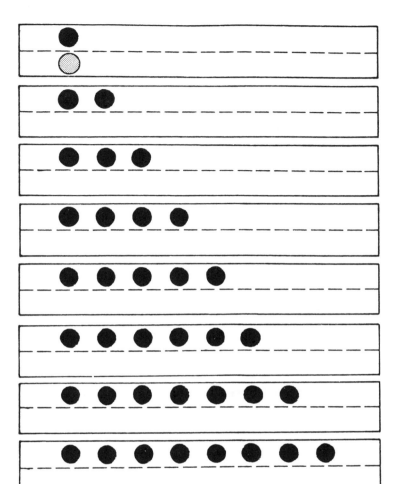

Double 1 is _____

Double 2 is _____

Double 3 is _____

Double 4 is _____

Double 5 is _____

Double ___ is _____

Double ___ is _____

Double ___ is _____

Draw more things to double the number in each picture.

Write the fact.

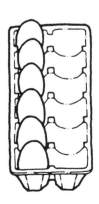  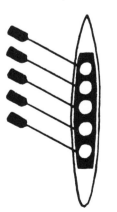 3+3=6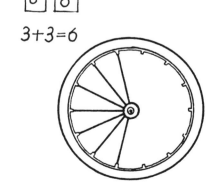

_____ _____ _____ _____

Ring the tens and ones.

6 tens 2 ones.

4 tens 8 ones.

2 tens 6 ones.

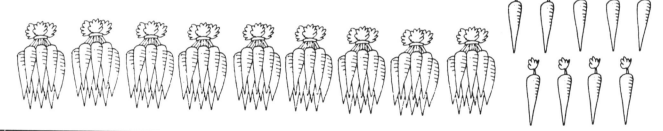

3 tens 5 ones.

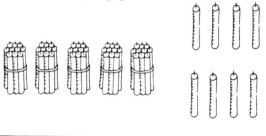

5 tens 4 ones.

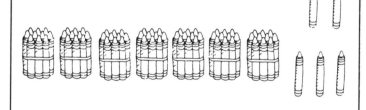

6 tens 3 ones.

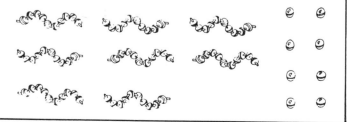

8 tens 7 ones.

Topic 17: Investigating Tens and Ones

Name _____

Count the tens. Write the number.

Count the ones. Write the number.

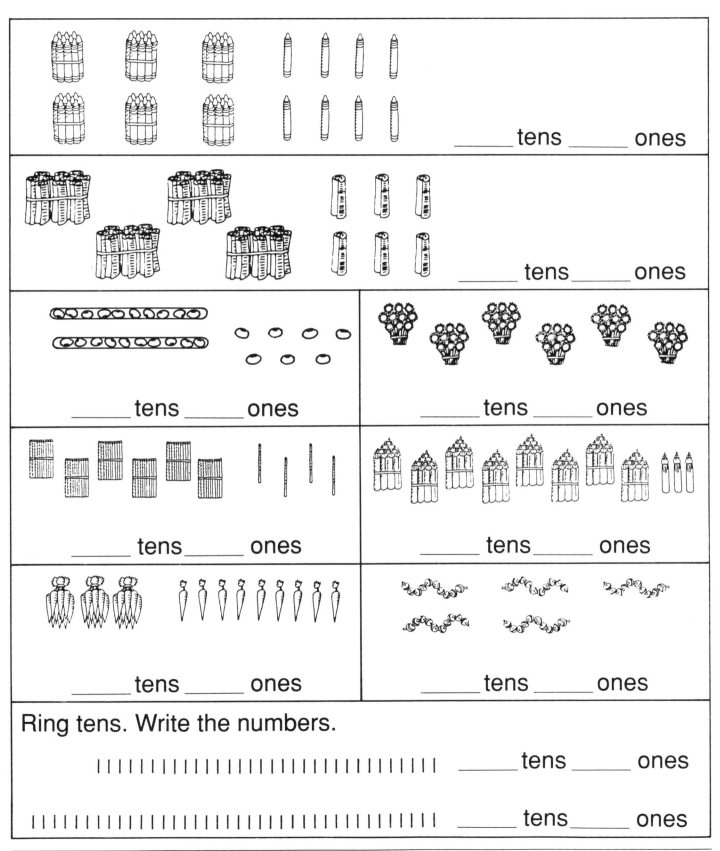

_____ tens _____ ones

_____ tens _____ ones

_____ tens _____ ones

_____ tens _____ ones

_____ tens _____ ones

_____ tens _____ ones

_____ tens _____ ones

_____ tens _____ ones

Ring tens. Write the numbers.

| | | | | | | | | | | | | | | | | | | | | | | | | | | | | | | | | _____ tens _____ ones

| | | | | | | | | | | | | | | | | | | | | | | | | | | | | | | | | | | _____ tens _____ ones

Name _____

For each pair of pictures, ring the tens in each number.
Put an X on the picture that shows the greater number.

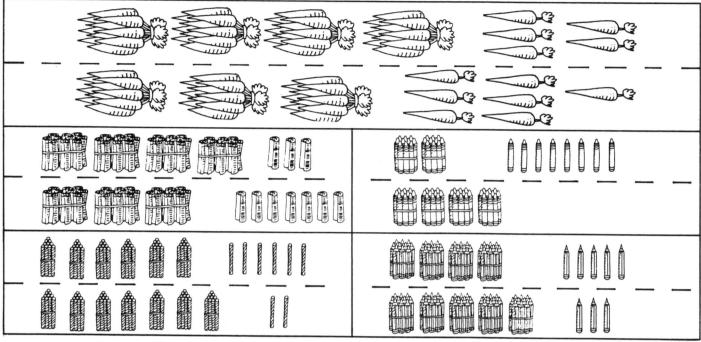

For each pair of pictures, write the numbers.
Put a check on the picture with the greater number.

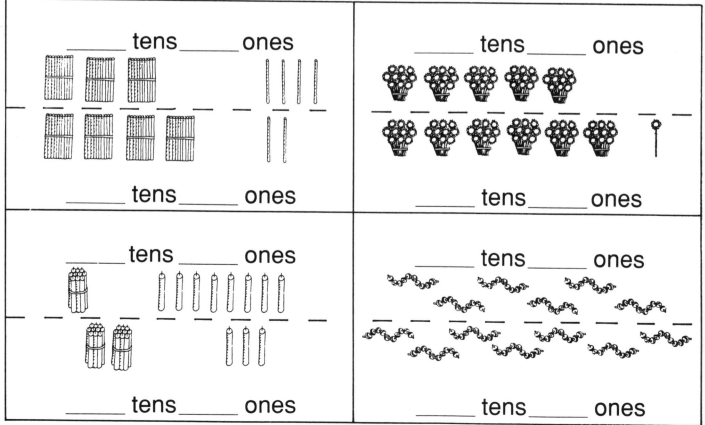

62

Name _____

Count the tens. Match with the correct number word.
Say the number.

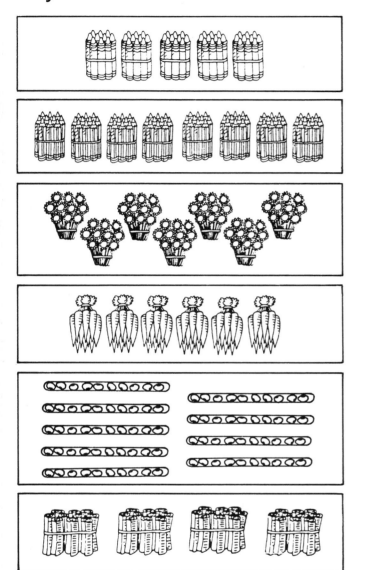

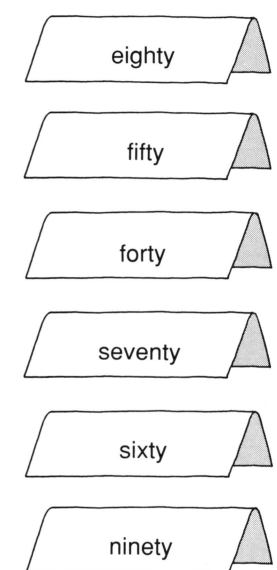

Ring groups of ten. Write the number word.

o oooooooooooooooooooooooooooooooo

o oooooooooooooooooooooooooooooooo _____

o ooooooooooooooooooooooooooooooooooooo

o oooooooooooooooooooooooooooooo _____

Name _____

Count the tens. Match with the correct number word.
Say the number.

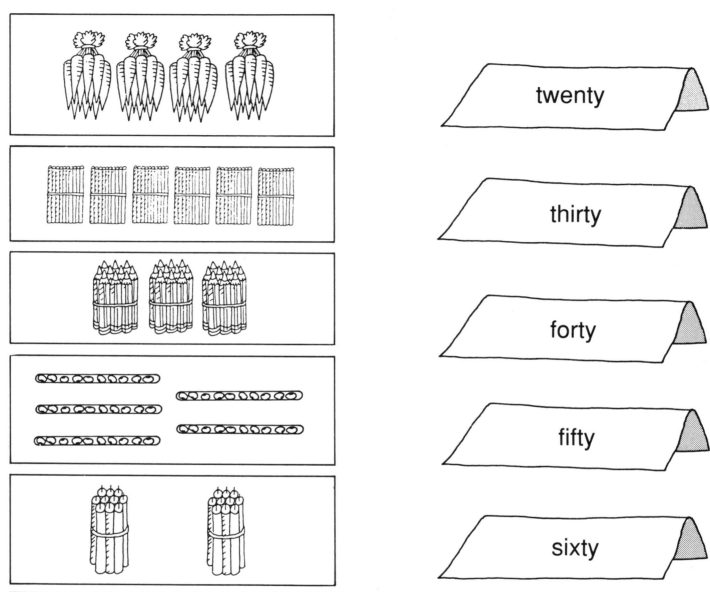

Ring groups of ten. Write the number word.

ooooooooooooooooooooo _____

oooooooooooooooooooooooooooooooo _____

ooooooooooooooooooooooooooooooo
ooooooooooooooooooooooooooooooo _____

Topic 17: Investigating Tens and Ones

Say the number. Ring tens to match.

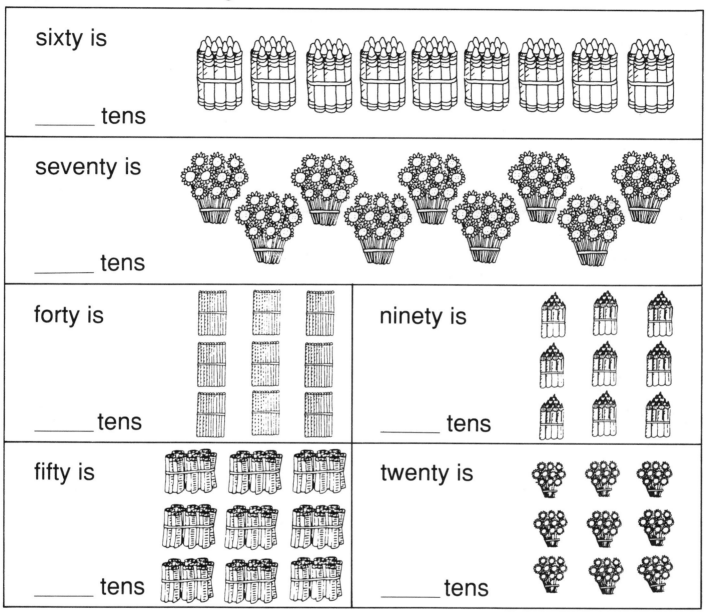

sixty is _____ tens	
seventy is _____ tens	
forty is _____ tens	ninety is _____ tens
fifty is _____ tens	twenty is _____ tens

Ring the tens. Write the number word.

\| \| \| \| \| \| \| \| \| \| \| \| \| \| \| \| \| \| \| \| \| \| \| \| \| \| \| \| \| \|

\| \| \| \| \| \| \| \| \| \| \| \| \| \| \| \| \| \| \| \| \| \| \| \| \| \| \| \| \| \|

\| \| \| \| \| \| \| \| \| \| \| \| \| \| \| \| \| \| \| \| \| \|

_____ | _____ | _____

Name _____

Say the number. Write how many tens.
Draw the tens.

twenty is __2__ tens

forty is _____ tens	eighty is _____ tens
seventy is _____ tens	fifty is _____ tens
thirty is _____ tens	sixty is _____ tens
twenty is _____ tens	ninety is _____ tens

Write the number word.

1 ten	2 tens	3 tens	4 tens
_____	_____	_____	_____

Topic 17: Investigating Tens and Ones

Name _____

Say the number. Write how many tens and ones.
Ring the tens and ones to match.

eighty-five	forty-two
_____ tens _____ ones	_____ tens _____ ones
seventy-three	sixty-eight
_____ tens _____ ones	_____ tens _____ ones

Draw tens and ones to match.

forty-six	sixty-four
_____ tens _____ ones	_____ tens _____ ones
sixty-two	forty-nine
_____ tens _____ ones	_____ tens _____ ones

Topic 17: Investigating Tens and Ones

Say the number. Write how many tens and ones.
Ring tens and ones to match.

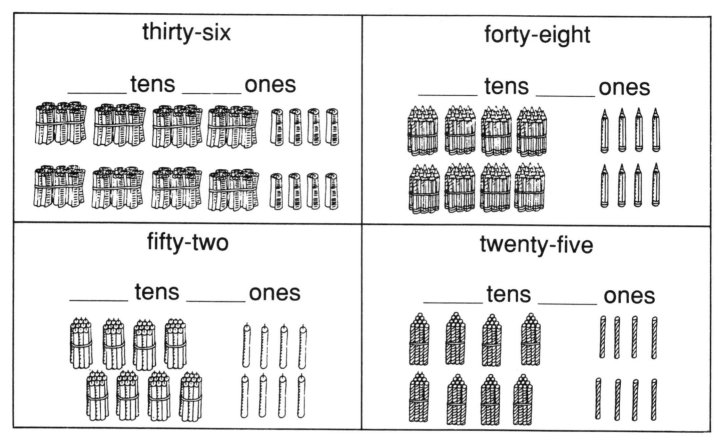

thirty-six	forty-eight
_____ tens _____ ones	_____ tens _____ ones
fifty-two	twenty-five
_____ tens _____ ones	_____ tens _____ ones

Draw tens and ones to match.

fifty-one	thirty-nine
_____ tens _____ ones	_____ tens _____ ones
twenty-three	thirty-two
_____ tens _____ ones	_____ tens _____ ones

68

Name _____

These numbers have just one ten.   (|||||||||) |||||| __seven__ teen

Count the ones. Say the number. Write the number word.

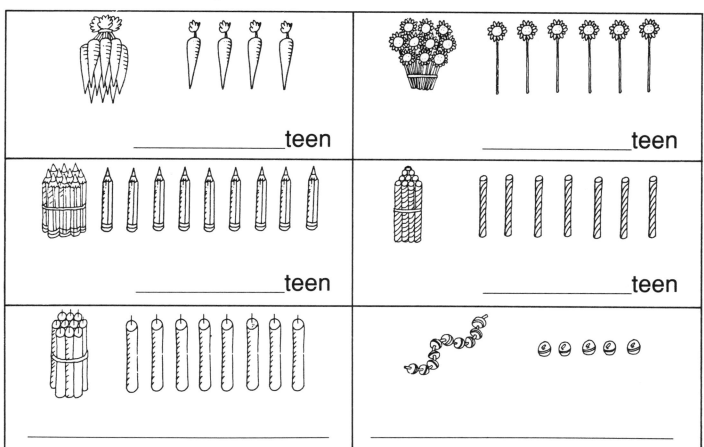

_____teen

_____teen

_____teen

_____teen

_____

_____

Draw a picture to show these numbers.

Use a ten and ones.

sixteen	nineteen
thirteen	fifteen

Name _____

Say the number.

Ring tens and ones to match.

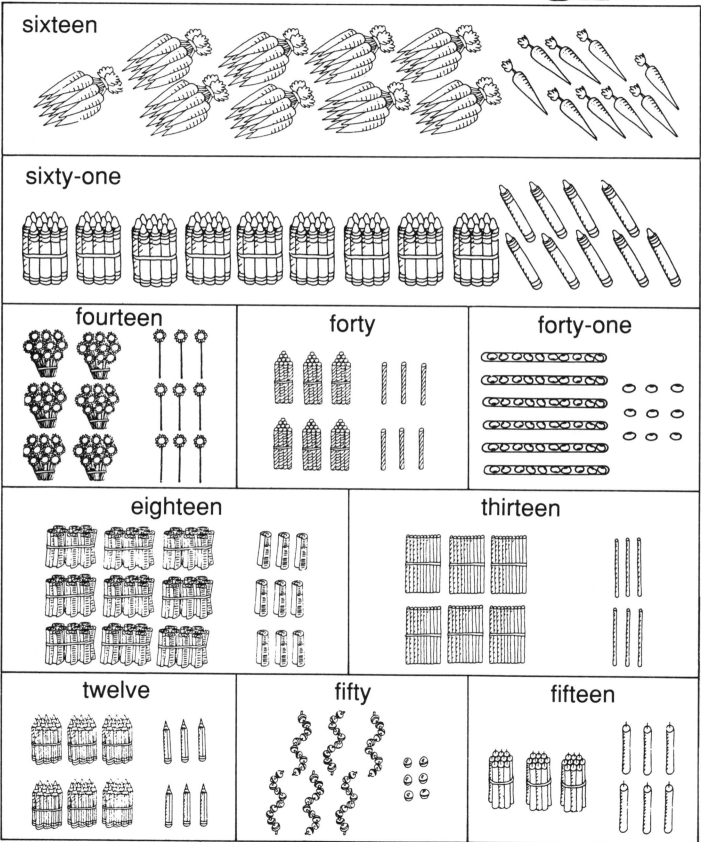

sixteen

sixty-one

fourteen

forty

forty-one

eighteen

thirteen

twelve

fifty

fifteen

70

Name _____

Draw a picture to match.
Write the number word.

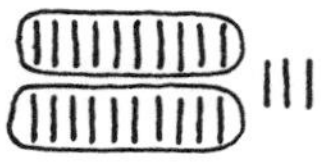

⬚⬚III twenty-three   tens | ones
                        2 | 3

| | tens | ones |
| | 3 | 4 |

_____

| | tens | ones |
| | 6 | 2 |

_____

| | tens | ones |
| | 7 | 1 |

_____

| | tens | ones |
| | 9 | 5 |

_____

| | tens | ones |
| | 4 | 9 |

_____

| | tens | ones |
| | 8 | 3 |

_____

Draw a picture for each number word.
Write how many tens and ones.

twenty-three ▦▦ ||| $\frac{\text{tens} | \text{ones}}{2 | 3}$

	tens	ones
fifty-three		

	tens	ones
forty-two		

	tens	ones
thirty-four		

	tens	ones
twenty-eight		

	tens	ones
sixteen		

	tens	ones
twelve		

Topic 18: Extending Place Value

Draw a picture for each number word.
Write how many tens and ones.

twenty (IIIIIIIII) (IIIIIIIII) tens | ones : 2 | 0

seventy-one	tens	ones

forty-nine	tens	ones

fifty	tens	ones

seventeen	tens	ones

fifteen	tens	ones

seventy	tens	ones

73

Name _____

Say the number.

Write how many tens and ones.

Color over the dots to match.

tens one twenty-one

2 1

thirty-two tens ones _____	forty-seven tens ones _____
thirteen _____	twenty-six _____
seventy-three _____	fifty-four _____
sixty-five _____	thirty-nine _____
ninety-three _____	seventeen _____
eighty-two _____	twelve _____

Topic 18: Extending Place Value

Name _____

Write a number for each story.
Draw a picture for each story.

I saw twenty-nine birds 29

| Dad cooked twenty-four hamburgers. | _____ |

| There are thirty-one children. | _____ |

| I collected forty-one cards. | _____ |

| Thirteen runners were in the race. | _____ |

| I took seventeen toys to school. | _____ |

| Grandma gave me fifteen cents. | _____ |

Name _____

Write how many tens.
Write how many ones.
Write the number.

 37
                      ___

3 tens 7 ones

_____ tens _____ ones	_____ tens _____ ones
_____ tens _____ ones	_____ tens _____ one
_____ tens _____ ones	_____ tens _____ ones
_____ tens _____ ones	_____ tens _____ ones
Draw a picture to match. **36** _____ _____ tens _____ ones	Draw a picture to match. **17** _____ _____ ten _____ ones

Topic 18: Extending Place Value

Write if the number inside the ring shows tens or ones.   5 ⑦
ones
___

(4) 6	(7) 2	8 (9)
_____	_____	_____
(3) 9	1 (7)	(2) 4
_____	_____	_____
(4) 0	(1) 9	6 (0)
_____	_____	_____

Ring the correct part of each number.

Write how many tens or ones.

5 2	6 1	2 5
_____ tens	_____ tens	_____ ones
3 7	4 6	5 2
_____ ones	_____ tens	_____ ones
9 4	1 4	3 0
_____ tens	_____ ones	_____ ones

Name _____

Write the missing numbers.

1	2	3	4	5	6	7	8	9	10
11	12	13	14		16	17	18	19	
21	22	23	24		26	27	28	29	
31	32	33	34		36	37	38	39	
41	42	43	44		46	47	48	49	
51	52	53	54		56	57	58	59	
61	62	63	64		66	67	68	69	
71	72	73	74		76	77	78	79	
81	82	83	84		86	87	88	89	
91	92	93	94		96	97	98	99	

Use red to color all the numbers with an 8 in the ones place.

Say these numbers.

Use orange to color all the numbers with a 3 in the ones place.

Say these numbers.

Use green to color all the numbers with a 2 in the tens place.

Say these numbers.

Use blue to color all the numbers with a 7 in the tens place.

Say these numbers.

Which numbers did you color twice? _____

Topic 18: Extending Place Value

For each pair of pictures, write the numbers.
Check the number that is greater.

			tens ones
			_____
			tens ones
			_____

	tens ones		tens ones
	_____		_____
	tens ones		tens ones
	_____		_____

	tens ones		tens ones
forty-two	_____	fifty-one	_____
	tens ones		tens ones
forty-six	_____	eighteen	_____

	tens ones		tens ones
eighty-two	_____	seventy-three	_____
	tens ones		tens ones
sixty-four	_____	seventy-eight	_____

	tens ones		tens ones
sixteen	_____	ninety	_____
	tens ones		tens ones
sixty	_____	eighty-eight	_____

Name _____

Write the missing numbers in each row.

42 43 44 __45__ ____ ____ ____ ____ ____ ____

66 67 68 ____ ____ ____ ____ , ____ ____

90 80 70 ____ ____ ____ ____ ____ ____

5 15 25 ____ ____ ____ ____ ____ ____

21 31 41 ____ ____ ____ ____ ____ ____

32 34 36 ____ ____ ____ ____ ____ ____

86 76 66 ____ ____ ____ ____ ____ ____

Put a X on the number that does not belong.

29	39	49	59	69	70	89	99
9	12	15	18	21	23	27	30
56	55	54	53	52	51	50	40

The number just after	The number just before	The number that is 10 more than
24 is _____	26 is _____	72 is _____
39 is _____	51 is _____	17 is _____
70 is _____	44 is _____	60 is _____
89 is _____	36 is _____	89 is _____

80

Name _____

Paste pictures of shapes that look the same.

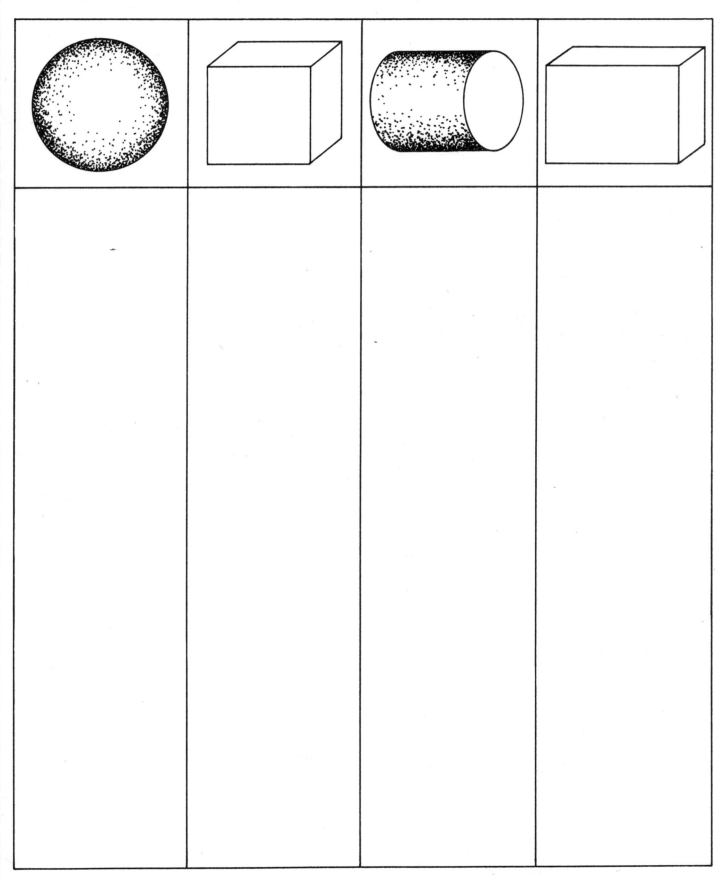

Name _____

Write the numbers. Fill in the number cards.
Color the fruit that is left.

Start with __7__ take away __2__

$$7 - 2$$

Start with _____ take away _____

Start with _____ take away _____

Start with _____ take away _____

Start with _____ take away _____

82

Name _____

Write the numbers.

Color the beans that are left. Write how many are left.

Start with ___7___

take away ___3___

7 − 3 ◁ is the same number as ▷ 4

Start with _____

take away _____

___ − ___ ◁ is the same number as ▷ _____

Start with _____

take away _____

___ − ___ ◁ is the same number as ▷ _____

Start with _____

take away _____

___ − ___ ◁ is the same number as ▷ _____

Topic 22: Subtraction Sentences

Name _____

Write the numbers. Color the oranges that are left.

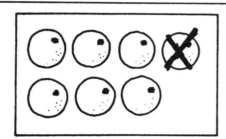 $7 - 1$ ⟨is equal to⟩ 6
_____ ⟨is equal to⟩ ___

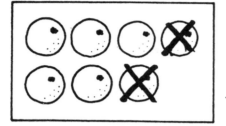 _____ ⟨is equal to⟩ ___

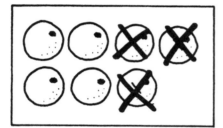 _____ ⟨is equal to⟩ ___

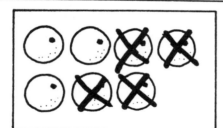 _____ ⟨is equal to⟩ ___

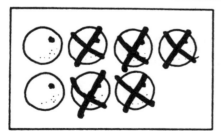 _____ ⟨is equal to⟩ ___

 _____ ⟨is equal to⟩ ___

Topic 22: Subtraction Sentences

Name _____

Add more drawings.

Write the number.

Start with 3 plants. Add more to make 8.	 3 + _____ is equal to 8.
Start with 1 egg. Add more to make 5.	 1 + _____ is equal to 5.
Start with 5 saucers. Add more to make 7.	 5 + _____ is equal to 7.
Start with 5 bowls. Add more to make 8.	 5 + _____ is equal to 8.
Start with 2 forks. Add more to make 8.	 2 + _____ is equal to 8.

Name _____

Color the animals you add or take. Write the numbers.

Start with 3. Add 4.

$$3 + 4 = 7$$

Start with 7. Take 4.

$$\underline{\quad} - \underline{\quad} = \underline{\quad}$$

Start with 4. Add 5.

$$\underline{\quad} + \underline{\quad} = \underline{\quad}$$

Start with 9. Take 5.

$$\underline{\quad} - \underline{\quad} = \underline{\quad}$$

Start with 2. Add 6.

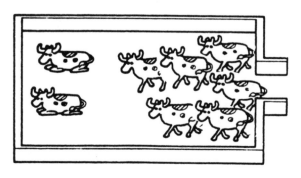

$$\underline{\quad} + \underline{\quad} = \underline{\quad}$$

Start with 8. Take 6.

$$\underline{\quad} - \underline{\quad} = \underline{\quad}$$

Topic 23: Relating Addition and Subtraction

Name _____

Match each stamp in a bottom row with the stamp above.

Color the stamps that are left over.

Write the numbers.

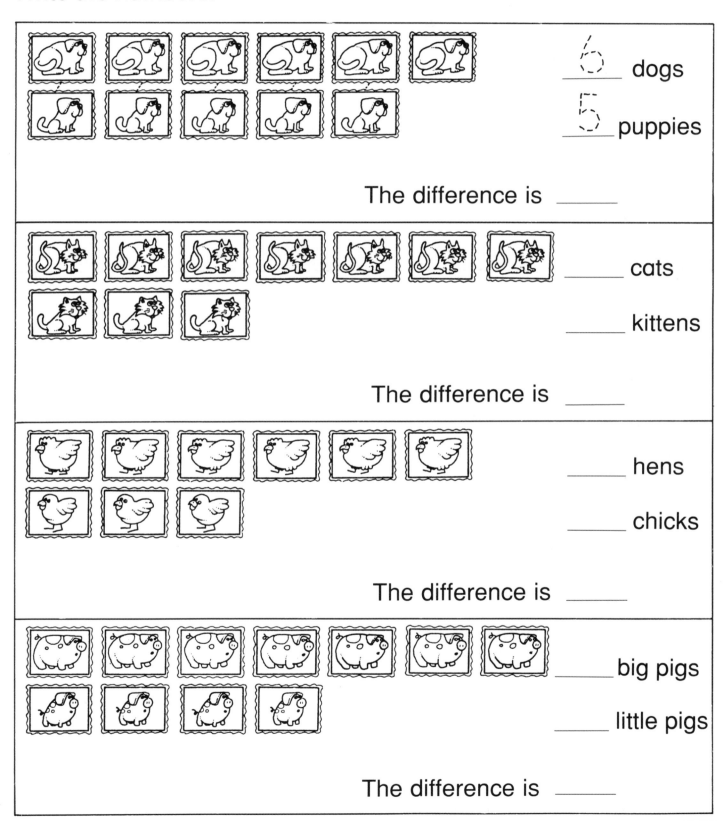

6 ____ dogs

5 ____ puppies

The difference is _____

____ cats

____ kittens

The difference is _____

____ hens

____ chicks

The difference is _____

____ big pigs

____ little pigs

The difference is _____

Name _____

Draw a picture to match each story.
Write a subtraction fact.

Four balls. ○ ○ $-\frac{4}{3}$
One rolls away ○ ⊗

Nine books . . . four fall down.	
Nine balls . . . one rolls away.	
Eight eggs . . . three break.	
Ten balloons . . . two go pop.	
Eleven cans . . . take two.	
Eight . . . subtract four.	

Topic 24: Subtraction Fact Strategies - count on and count back

Name _____

Write what you see happening.
Count back. Write the answer.

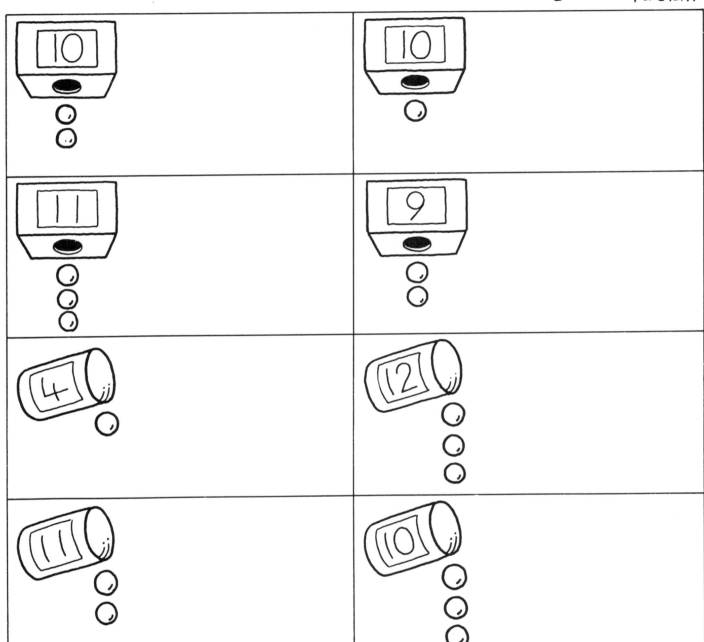

Write the answers.

5	8	6	7	8	7	8
−1	−1	−3	−1	−2	−3	−2

Name _____

Draw dots on each domino to match the addition fact.

Complete each addition fact.

Write 2 subtraction facts for each domino.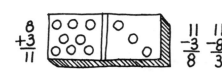

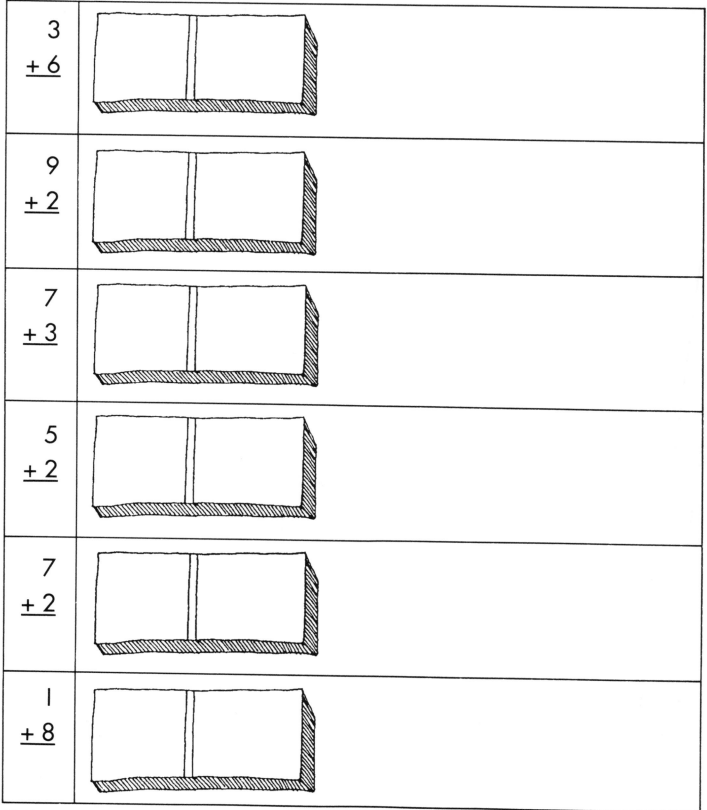

$$\begin{array}{r} 3 \\ +6 \\ \hline \end{array}$$

$$\begin{array}{r} 9 \\ +2 \\ \hline \end{array}$$

$$\begin{array}{r} 7 \\ +3 \\ \hline \end{array}$$

$$\begin{array}{r} 5 \\ +2 \\ \hline \end{array}$$

$$\begin{array}{r} 7 \\ +2 \\ \hline \end{array}$$

$$\begin{array}{r} 1 \\ +8 \\ \hline \end{array}$$

Topic 24: Subtraction Fact Strategies - count on and count back

Name _____

Complete each addition fact.

Draw a picture to match.

Write some other facts to match the picture.

$\begin{array}{r} 4 \\ +3 \\ \hline 7 \end{array}$ $\begin{array}{r} 3 \\ +4 \\ \hline 7 \end{array}$ $\begin{array}{r} 7 \\ -3 \\ \hline 4 \end{array}$ $\begin{array}{r} 7 \\ -4 \\ \hline 3 \end{array}$

$\begin{array}{r} 2 \\ +7 \\ \hline \end{array}$	
$\begin{array}{r} 6 \\ +3 \\ \hline \end{array}$	
$\begin{array}{r} 5 \\ +3 \\ \hline \end{array}$	
$\begin{array}{r} 8 \\ +3 \\ \hline \end{array}$	
$\begin{array}{r} 2 \\ +6 \\ \hline \end{array}$	

Name _____

Fill in the empty boxes. Draw a picture of your change.

I have	10¢
I spend	
My change is	
My change in coins	

4¢

I have	10¢
I spend	
My change is	
My change in coins	

6¢

I have	10¢
I spend	
My change is	
My change in coins	

7¢

I have	10¢
I spend	
My change is	
My change in coins	

5¢

Topic 25: Problem Solving with Money

Name _____

Write how much change you get. Draw a picture of your change.

I have	I buy	My change is	My change in coins
ONE DIME	pen 8¢	2¢	◯ ◯
ONE DIME	apple 4¢		
ONE DIME	pencil 2¢		
ONE DIME	cherries 5¢		
ONE DIME	pear 7¢		

Name _____

Pat and Terry filled some containers with water.

This is the graph they made.

**Number
of
paper cups
full**

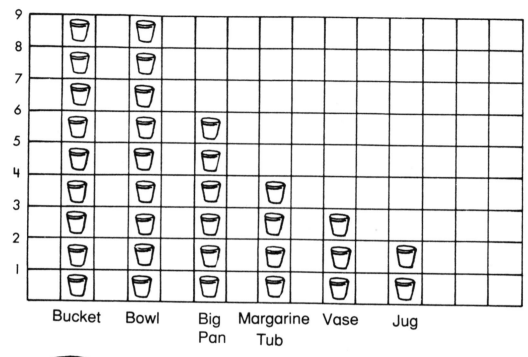

Measure some containers. Make your own graph.

Topic 26: Measurement - capacity

Name _____

The cards tell the place of each car in the race.

Match each card to the correct car.

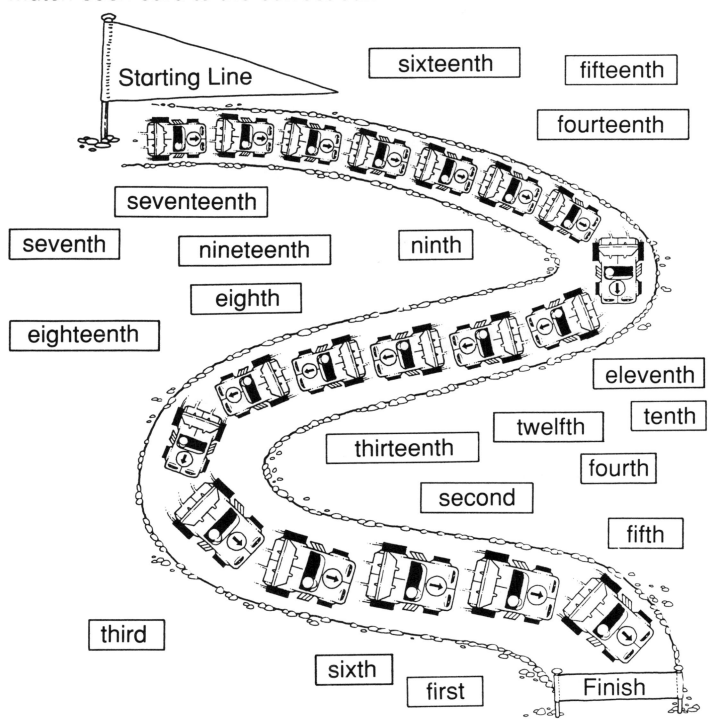

Starting Line

sixteenth

fifteenth

fourteenth

seventeenth

seventh

nineteenth

ninth

eighth

eighteenth

eleventh

tenth

twelfth

thirteenth

fourth

second

fifth

third

sixth

first

Finish

Use red to color the car that is just after the twelfth car.

Use blue to color the car that is just before the sixteenth car.

Use green to color the car that is just before the eleventh car.

Name _____

How many shapes are in each row? _____
Complete each take-away sentence.

✿ ✿ ✿ ✿ ✿ ✿ ✿ ✿ ✿ ✿ ✿ ✿ ✿ ✖ $14 - 1 =$ _____

❄ ❄ ❄ ❄ ❄ ❄ ❄ ❄ ❄ ❄ ❄ ❄ ✖ ✖ $14 - 2 =$ _____

● ● ● ● ● ● ● ● ● ● ● ✖ ✖ ● $14 - 3 =$ _____

▢ ▢ ▢ ▢ ▢ ▢ ▢ ▢ ▢ ▢ ⊠ ⊠ ⊠⊠ $14 - 4 =$ _____

❖ ❖ ❖ ❖ ❖ ❖ ❖ ❖ ❖ ✖ ✖ ✖✖ ✖ $14 - 5 =$ _____

♣ ♣ ♣ ♣ ♣ ♣ ♣ ♣ ✖ ✖ ✖ ✖ ✖ ✖ $14 - 6 =$ _____

☆ ☆ ☆ ☆ ☆ ☆ ☆ ✖ ✖ ✖ ✖ ✖ ✖ ✖ $14 - 7 =$ _____

Cross out the shapes to keep the pattern going.
Write a take-away sentence each time.

_____

_____

_____

_____

Write the answers.

4	14	4	14	4	14	4	14
-1	-1	-2	-2	-3	-3	-4	-4

Topic 27: Investigating Two-Digit Numbers

Name _____

Color 10 beads in each row.
Then complete the number sentences.

$8 + 6 = 14$ $8 + 2 + 4 = 14$ $10 + 4 = 14$

$8 + \_\_\_ = 15$ $8 + 2 + \_\_\_ = 15$ $10 + \_\_\_ = 15$

$8 + \_\_\_ = 16$ $8 + 2 + \_\_\_ = 16$ $10 + \_\_\_ = 16$

$8 + \_\_\_ = 17$ $8 + 2 + \_\_\_ = 17$ $10 + \_\_\_ = 17$

$8 + \_\_\_ = 18$ $8 + 2 + \_\_\_ = 18$ $10 + \_\_\_ = 18$

$8 + \_\_\_ = 19$ $8 + 2 + \_\_\_ = 19$ $10 + \_\_\_ = 19$

Write the answers.

$7 + 3 + 4 = \_\_\_$ $8 + 2 + 3 = \_\_\_$ $9 + 1 + 7 = \_\_\_$

$8 + 2 + 2 = \_\_\_$ $9 + 1 + 8 = \_\_\_$ $7 + 3 + 7 = \_\_\_$

Name _____

Estimate first, then use a pan balance to weigh.
Write the numbers.

The children will need the items listed for measuring.

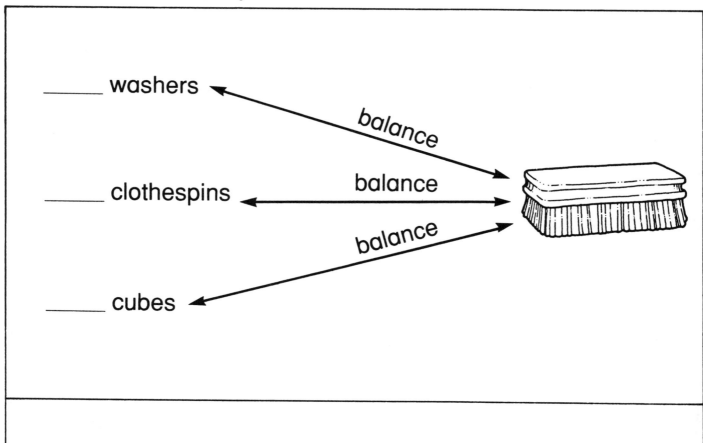

_____ washers

_____ clothespins

_____ cubes

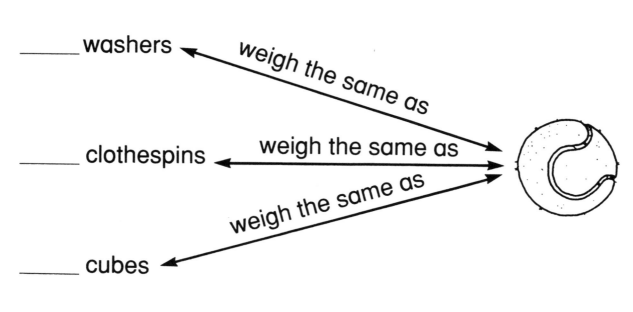

_____ washers

_____ clothespins

_____ cubes

Topic 28: Measurement - weight

Name _____

Write how many washers are needed
to balance each object.

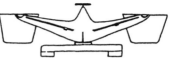

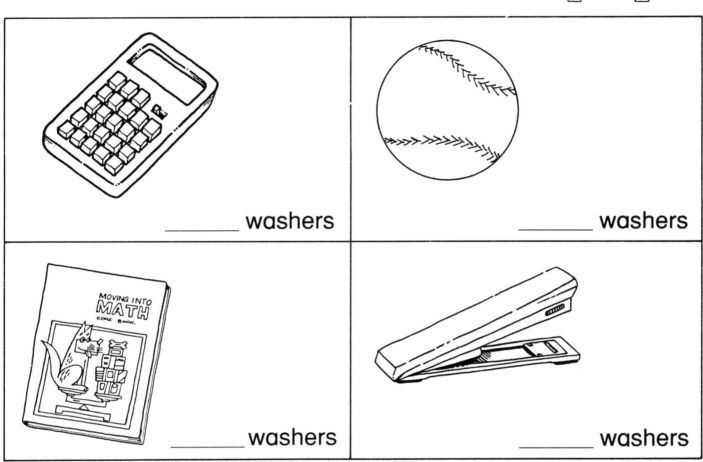

_____ washers

_____ washers

_____ washers

_____ washers

The children will need the items listed for measuring.

Draw or write the answers.

The _____ needed the most washers.

The _____ needed the fewest washers.

The _____ and the _____

needed about the same number of washers.

The _____ weighed _____ washers more

than the _____.

Name _____

Balance some objects like these against a one-kilogram weight.

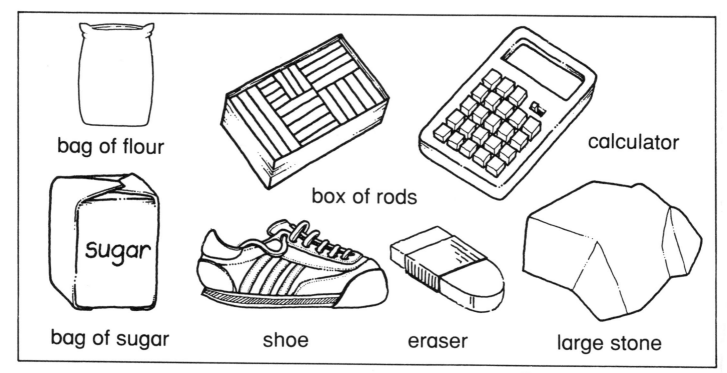

bag of flour

box of rods

calculator

bag of sugar

shoe

eraser

large stone

The children will need items for measuring.

Write the name of each object you weigh.

Check the correct column.

Object	More than 1 kilogram	Equal to 1 kilogram	Less than 1 kilogram

Name _____

Color shapes with 2 equal parts red.

Color shapes with 4 equal parts blue.

Name _____

Check the shapes that show 2 equal parts.
Color one half of those shapes red.

Topic 29: Area and Fractions

Color one half of each shape that is divided into 2 equal parts.

Cover each whole strip with 2 rods of equal length.

Put the rods end-to-end | Cuisenaire rods

Color one half of each strip the same color
as the rod you used to cover it.

Cut out some paper squares.

Fold them into 2 halves in different ways.

Paste them here.

Make your squares
about the same size
as these.

Color one fourth of each shape that is divided into 4 equal parts.

Cut a paper strip as long as your handspan.

Fold it into 4 equal parts.

Color one fourth of the strip red.

Paste the strip here.

Cut out 3 paper squares the same size as these.

Fold them into 4 equal parts, in different ways.

Color each fourth a different color.

Paste your
squares here.

Cut out 2 paper squares the same size as these.

Fold them into 4 equal parts, in different ways.

Color 1 fourth      Color 3 fourths

Topic 29: Area and Fractions

Name _____

Estimate, then cover each shape with squares this size:
Write a number on each shape to tell how many
squares you used.

Name _____

Draw 2 cherries on each plate. Write the numbers.

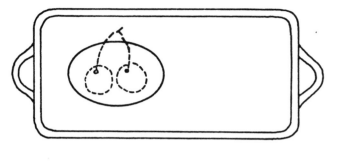

__1__ pair of __2__

_____ cherries in all

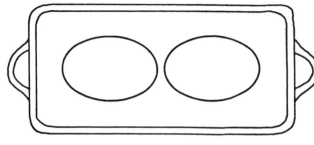

_____ pair of __2__

_____ cherries in all

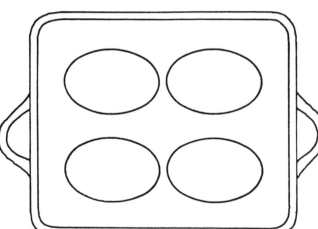

_____ pairs of _____

_____ cherries in all

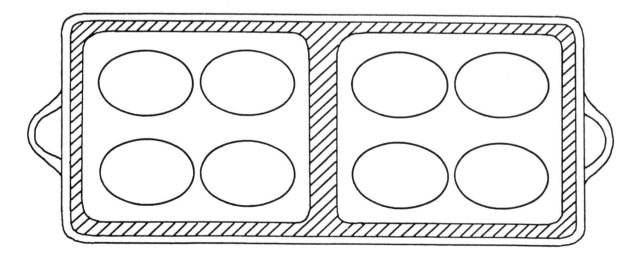

_____ pairs of _____   _____ cherries in all

Topic 30: Investigating Multiplication and Division

Name _____

Draw rings. Write the numbers.

Ring each pair of boots.

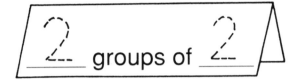
2 groups of 2

Ring each bundle of ties.

_____ bundles of _____

Ring each bunch of flowers.

_____ bunches of _____

Ring each group of shells.

_____ groups of _____

Name _____

Ring each group.

Count how many things there are in each group.

Write the numbers.

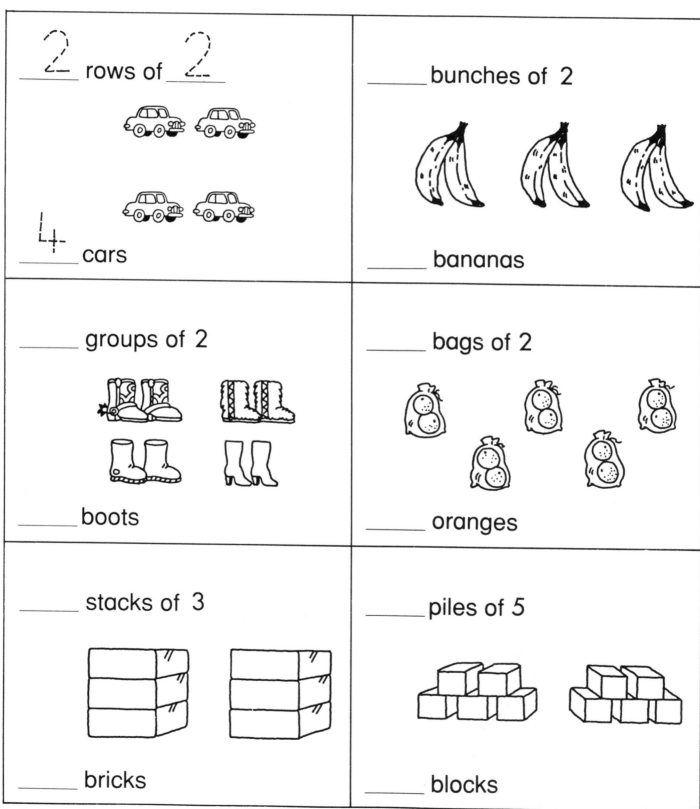

_2_ rows of _2_

_4_ cars

_____ bunches of 2

_____ bananas

_____ groups of 2

_____ boots

_____ bags of 2

_____ oranges

_____ stacks of 3

_____ bricks

_____ piles of 5

_____ blocks

Topic 30: Investigating Multiplication and Division

Name _____

Ring each group.

Count how many things there are in each group.

Write the numbers.

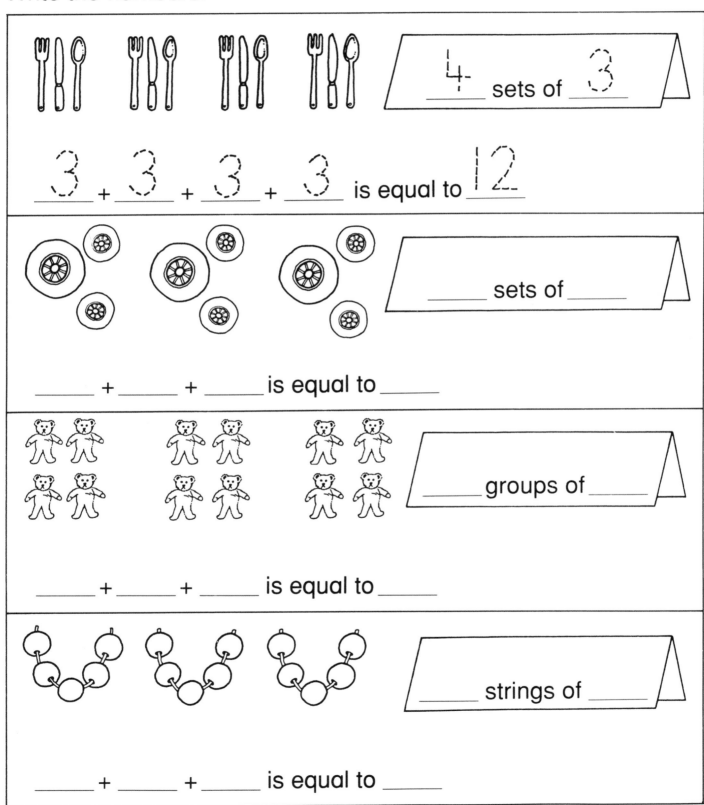

_4_ sets of _3_

_3_ + _3_ + _3_ + _3_ is equal to _12_

_____ sets of _____

_____ + _____ + _____ is equal to _____

_____ groups of _____

_____ + _____ + _____ is equal to _____

_____ strings of _____

_____ + _____ + _____ is equal to _____

Draw 12 buttons in each space.

Ring each group of 2.

There are _____ groups of 2.

Ring each group of 3.

There are _____ groups of 3.

Ring each group of 4.

There are _____ groups of 4.

Ring each group of 6.

There are _____ groups of 6.

Topic 30: Investigating Multiplication and Division

Name _____

Count how many. Write the number.

Ring groups of 2. Write the number of groups.

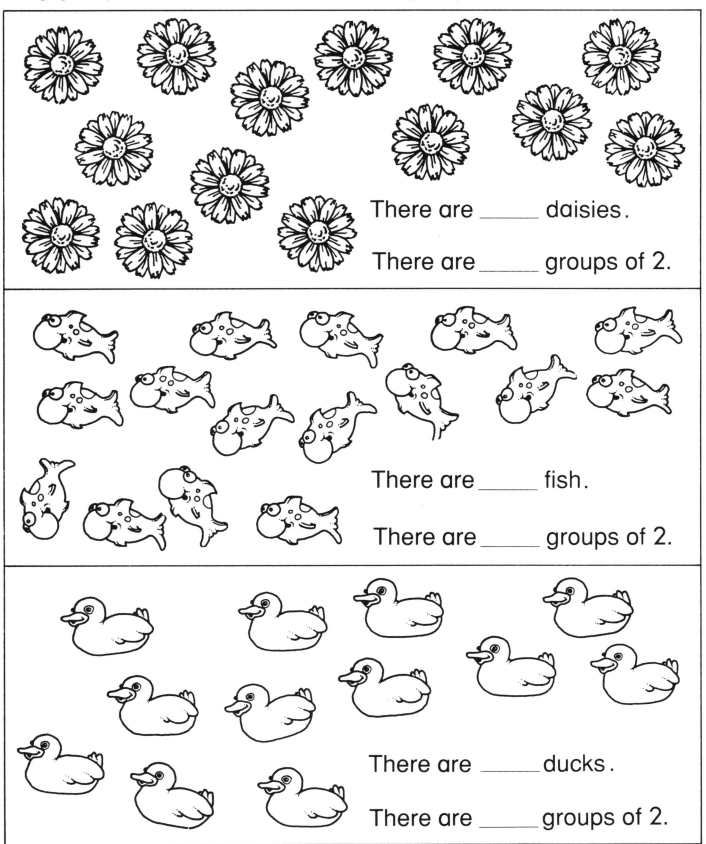

There are _____ daisies.

There are _____ groups of 2.

There are _____ fish.

There are _____ groups of 2.

There are _____ ducks.

There are _____ groups of 2.

Name _____

Put a bean on each ◯.

Share the beans among the bunnies.

Write the numbers.

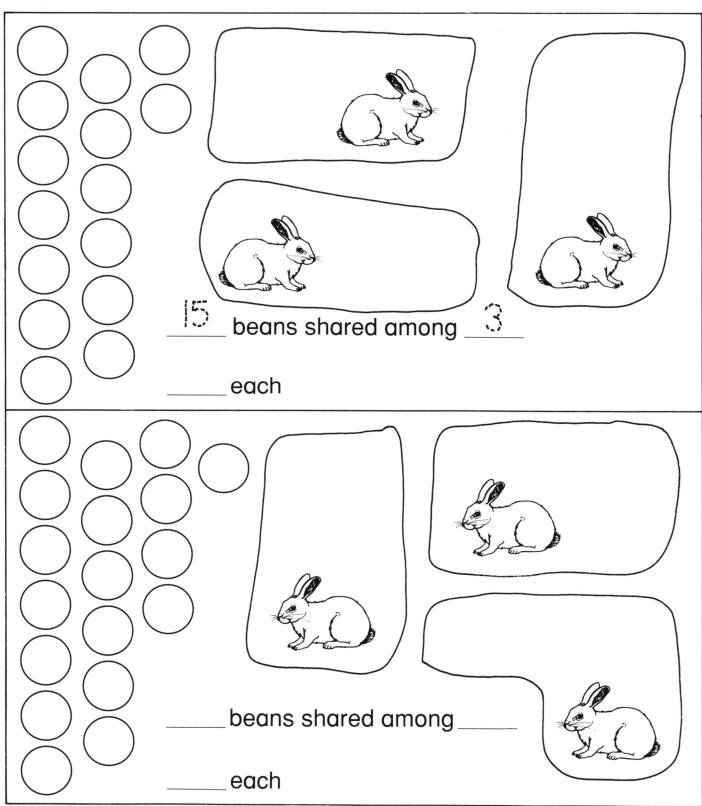

15 beans shared among 3

_____ each

_____ beans shared among _____

_____ each

Topic 30: Investigating Multiplication and Division